Run the Alps'
TRAIL RUNNING CHAMONIX MONT BLANC
30 Must-Do Trail Runs in France, Switzerland, and Italy

With gratitude for those who pioneered and inspired trail running in the region around Mont Blanc, and in particular, Bruno Brunod, Georges Costaz, Jean-Michel Lenta, Giorgio Simonetti, and Christian Roussel.

Run the Alps' Trail Running Chamonix Mont Blanc:
30 Must-Do Trail Runs in France, Switzerland, and Italy

Graphic design: Daniel Malak
Cover design: Chloé Châtelain based on a previous cover illustration by Timothy Hall
Editor: Sonia Curtis

ISBN: 978-3-03964-037-9
First edition: June 2024
Printed in the Czech Republic

Avenue des Acacias 7
1006 Lausanne
Switzerland

helvetiq.com

MIX
Paper from responsible sources
FSC® C014138

Run the Alps'
TRAIL RUNNING CHAMONIX MONT BLANC
30 Must-Do Trail Runs in France, Switzerland, and Italy

MAP

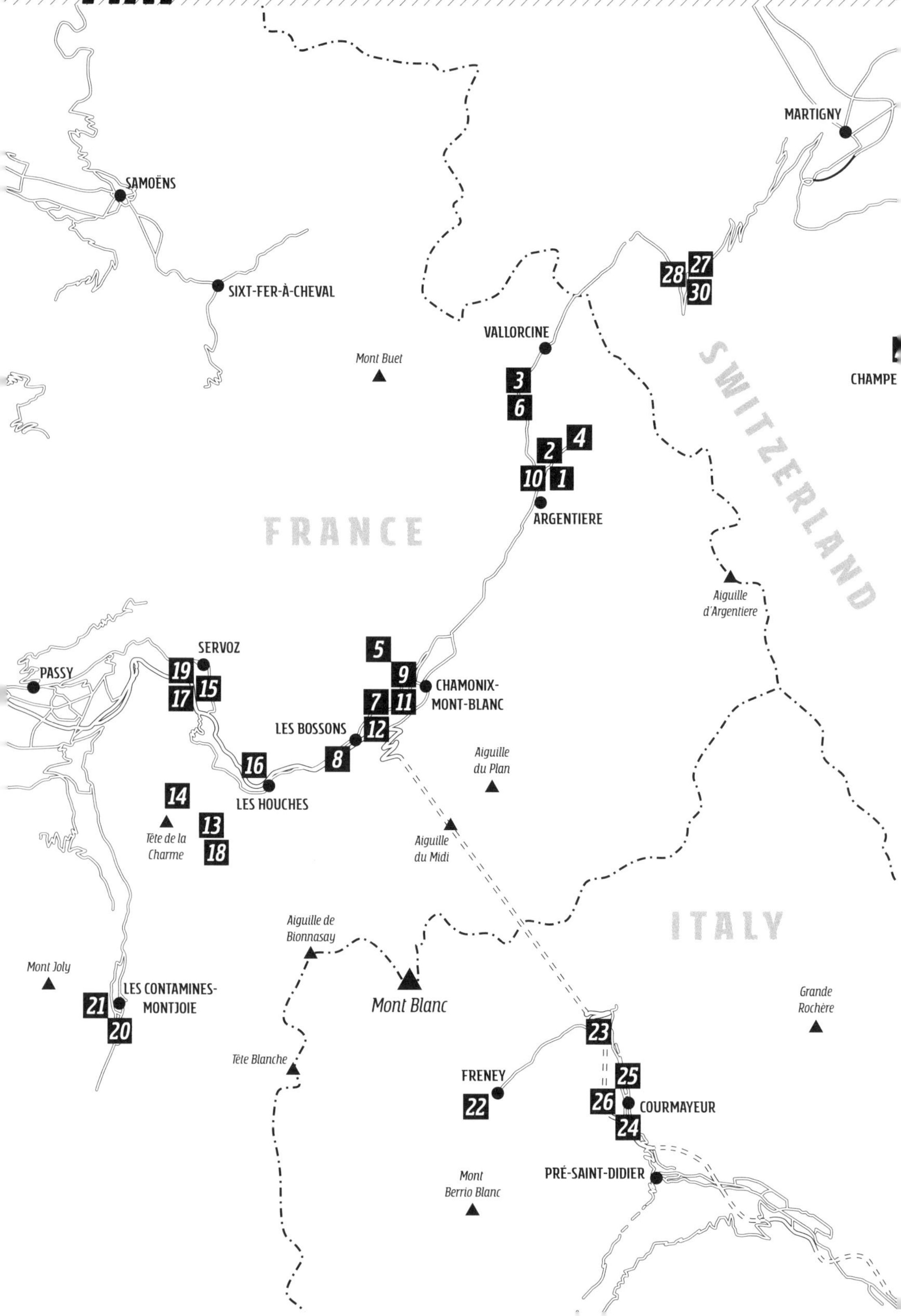

SAMOËNS
SIXT-FER-À-CHEVAL
MARTIGNY
28
27
30
VALLORCINE
Mont Buet
SWITZERLAND
CHAMPE
3
6
4
2
10
1
ARGENTIERE
FRANCE
Aiguille d'Argentiere
5
SERVOZ
9
PASSY
19
15
17
CHAMONIX-MONT-BLANC
7
11
LES BOSSONS
12
8
Aiguille du Plan
16
LES HOUCHES
14
13
18
Tête de la Charme
Aiguille du Midi
ITALY
Aiguille de Bionnasay
Mont Joly
LES CONTAMINES-MONTJOIE
21
20
Mont Blanc
Grande Rochère
23
Tête Blanche
25
FRENEY
22
26
COURMAYEUR
24
Mont Berrio Blanc
PRÉ-SAINT-DIDIER

CONTENTS

This guide was conceived and produced by Run the Alps. Our mission is to share and celebrate trail running in the Alps. We do that by creating and sharing content—for example, the book you have in your hands—and through offering trail running tours around the Alps. For more information, please visit us at runthealps.com, where you can also download GPX tracks for these routes.

INTRODUCTION

Welcome

Welcome to the Mont Blanc region, undeniably the world's epicenter of trail running and home to a rich network of interconnecting trails that thread their way through three countries and around the Mont Blanc massif. Here, mountain life is not a subculture; it is *the* culture. The mayor of Chamonix is an accomplished trail runner, and the current holder of the women's Fastest Known Time up and down Mont Blanc lives in the mountain's shadow (and is a key contributor to this guide!).

Race participation is booming, and Fastest Known Times are being set and reset. New running and mountaineering ventures, both commercial and nonprofit, are springing up everywhere. And all around, the trails are abuzz with the energy of trail runners pushing personal boundaries or simply reinvigorating themselves with a break from their daily routines.

About this guide

This guide is for every trail runner, no matter your fitness or skill level. We've worked hard to meet you where you are and provide you with a wealth of memorable and rewarding running experiences in this wonderful region. We hope this guide helps to open a door for those curious about the sport, and opens the door to adventure wider for those who have already discovered how trail running can change your life.

What's online?

Trail Running Chamonix Mont Blanc is more than just the copy in your hands. It comes with an online component, available at runthealps.com/routes. Here you'll find downloadable GPX files for each run, and if significant, permanent changes are made to a route, we'll post them there. You'll also find a wealth of additional information: stories, in-depth guides to towns, other trail running books you might like, our favorite apps, and even information on how to hire a trail running guide.

Trail running in the Mont Blanc region

In Chamonix and elsewhere in the Alps, moving quickly along mountain trails has been part of the mountain culture for decades.

Since the 1970s, it has passed through various branding and rebranding moments: *Dynamique Walk*, *La Marche Nordique*, and—more recently—simply, *le trail*.

In August 1978, with ultra-distance trail running gaining adherents around the world, two Chamonix climbers, Christian Roussel and Jacky Duc, raised the profile of such efforts for residents around the Mont Blanc massif. Using a combination of roads and trails, the duo ran around Mont Blanc without support, completing the loop in a remarkably speedy 24:45.

A few years later, just after the inaugural Cross du Mont Blanc race, Roussel played an instrumental part in starting Chamonix's running club, Chamonix Mont-Blanc Marathon (CMBM). The organization combined running on roads with running on trails. In the Chamonix valley, however, arguably the strongest driver of trail running would become the Ultra-Trail du Mont-Blanc (UTMB), which captured the imagination of locals already curious about trail and ultra running. Together, the growing interest in running on trails and the dramatic new ultra-race created a wave of activity.

In other locations around Mont Blanc, trail running developed more or less in parallel, though with notable differences. In Courmayeur and throughout the Aosta valley, small groups of runners had informally used the trails for years, just as they had on the French side of the mountain. Some brought their speed to mountainous, off-trail routes, pioneering what would become known as Skyrunning.

Today, there's a steady drumbeat of trail running around the region. In Chamonix, CMBM continues to be one of the driving forces, with more than 250 members and several paid coaches. It hosts social events and twice-weekly training sessions for all levels and ages, and it oversees the popular Trail des Aiguilles Rouges races.

Chamonix, in particular, is having a moment. While longtime annual events like the Climbing World Cup and Kandahar Alpine Ski Racing have historically brought in tens of thousands of visitors, according to the town's tourist office, the valley now welcomes well over 100,000 trail runners annually—more than either climbers or skiers.

The valley is such a catalyst for trail running that enthusiasts are moving to Chamonix from around the world—a trend arguably started by Kilian Jornet, who lived in Chamonix for a number of years. During his time here, Jornet ticked off several fastest-known times, including the fastest time up and down Mont Blanc. He completed the route in 4 hours, 57 minutes, and 40 seconds—shaving 13 minutes off the previous record, which had stood for 23 years.

Trail racing in the Mont Blanc region

The Mont Blanc region is internationally known for a number of marquee trail races. In Chamonix, the most notable of these are the Mont-Blanc Marathon series of eight races and UTMB Mont-Blanc, which has expanded to nine events. On the other side of Mont Blanc is Gran Trail Courmayeur, with its three distances, and TORX, with five races, including the epic 450-kilometer Tor des Glaciers.

Trail racing here has deep roots that extend all the way back to the morning of August 8th, 1897, when ten guides from Chamonix's Compagnie des Guides gathered on the steps of the Saint Michel church. Their objective? A mountain race up and down the Brévent.

It was, as far as historians can tell, the region's first trail race. The winner that day, well over a century ago, was one Édouard Payot, who completed the route in two hours—a remarkably fast time, given the period, the gear he had, and the trail conditions, which must have been much rougher than they are now.

Trail racing here did not develop in isolation, however. Mountain running races came into their own in the Alps in the 1970s, with events like Trail des Dents du Midi and Sierre-Zinal in Switzerland. In this region, the Nid d'Aigle race in Saint-Gervais, first run in 1986, was one of those early pioneering races. These events were generally short, fast, and highly competitive.

Chamonix's 23-kilometer Cross du Mont-Blanc was first held during this era, in 1979. The race began under the auspices of the Club Alpin Français (CAF). Two years later, the CMBM took it over, and it was eventually passed to the Club des Sports in 1991. That first edition also featured a 13-kilometer race, but it was the Cross du Mont-Blanc that endured. Today, the race still follows much the same course. The event itself has grown enormously, and now includes a wide range of races, offering everything from a Vertical Kilometer race to a 90-kilometer epic around the Chamonix valley. A marathon was added in 2003, which is now the centerpiece of the long weekend and attracts top international racers.

At the turn of the century, Michel Poletti and others (see photo of Michel Poletti (left) and René Bachelard) in the town's CMBM running club were increasingly drawn toward running on trails. With its sense of adventure, trail running promoted self-sufficiency and a vibe that was less about competition and more about personal discovery and inclusivity—about finishing rather than winning. Then, in 2002, René Bachelard, President of CMBM, pushed to make a complete race around Mont Blanc a reality. Poletti and Bachelard organized a meeting and planning got underway.

The idea of a 100-mile race around Western Europe's highest point was daring, but thanks to Roussel and Duc, Bachelard and Poletti knew it was possible. The logistics were daunting. Some of the modern-day Tour du Mont-Blanc, such as the section between Rifugio Bertone and Rifugio Bonatti above Courmayeur, had not even been built. The effort came to fruition in 2003, with the first edition of what became known as UTMB Mont-Blanc. Seven hundred twenty runners participated—a number that far exceeded expectations.

Meanwhile, over on the other side of Mont Blanc, trail racing was also rapidly evolving. "Martze a pià," short and fast races of 10 to 15 kilometers that combined road and trail, started to take place in the Aosta valley at the end of the 1960s. There was little technical gear in those days, and early participants recall training after work in everyday pants and sneakers. Many villages had their own competitions. A number of these small local races continue to this day.

For decades, the trails around Courmayeur have been home to mountain runners who moved quickly off trail into exposed, alpine settings.

Less airy trail racing was inaugurated more formally in 2006, when the Mayor of Courmayeur asked residents to help organize the Italian section of the UTMB course from Col de la Seigne to Grand Col Ferret. In time, this group coalesced into the nonprofit Courmayeur Trailers Association.

In 2007, the region welcomed the first 100-kilometer trail race entirely within Italy, Trail Valdigne. The course passed through small villages in the shadow of Mont Blanc, finishing in Courmayeur. Then, in 2012, Courmayeur Trailers launched the three-distance event, Gran Trail Courmayeur.

Today, a cornucopia of races exists around the Mont Blanc region. While Chamonix and Courmayeur are the hotspots, other villages have their own trail running and racing spirit, with many smaller races proliferating that are constantly evolving.

USING THIS GUIDE

Trail Running Chamonix Mont Blanc is not meant to be used as a definitive or exclusive source of information. Anyone undertaking the runs listed in this book is solely responsible for their own safety, and should exercise good mountain judgment, undertake thorough route research, be physically and mentally ready for the challenges, be properly equipped, and be ready to turn back if conditions become more challenging than their abilities can handle. And when you do head out the door, always tell someone where you are going.

Picking the right run for you

This guide has divided the region around Mont Blanc into six distinct zones:

- Upper Chamonix Valley and Vallorcine, France
- Chamonix, France
- Lower Chamonix Valley, France
- Les Contamines, France
- Northern Aosta, Italy
- Valais, Switzerland

We've divided the runs into three difficulty levels, with 1 being the easiest and 3 the most challenging. We take into account four factors: distance, ascent, descent, and technical difficulty. We graded each of these four elements from one to three and calculated an average for the run.

Distance:
- 1 = <15 kilometers
- 2 = 15–25 kilometers
- 3 = >25 kilometers

Ascent and descent:
- 1 = <700 meters
- 2 = 700–1500 meters
- 3 = >1500 meters

Technical difficulty:
- 1 = easy
- 2 = rough terrain
- 3 = some scrambling and/or fixed equipment, such as cables or chains

What to bring

What you bring on your run will vary according to the route, season, conditions, and weather. For the shorter runs, typically graded 1, you may not need to take anything if the weather forecast is good, you're used to running in the mountains, and you'll pass a reliable water source. However, in the interest of caution and good mountain safety practices, we generally recommend taking a trail running vest with the following items:

- minimum of 500 ml water
- water filter for your flask (Though much of the fountain water in the alps is good to drink, it's never a bad idea to filter your water on the trail.)
- waterproof jacket (and pants if rain is forecast)
- cap or hat, sunglasses, and sunscreen
- food
- phone
- cash
- trail running poles
- small first aid kit

This is what we consider a bare minimum. If you are new to trail running, the weather forecast is uncertain, or you have any other concerns, consider adding such items as a warm top and bottom layer, a backup battery for your phone, and other items that add to your security on the trails.

Bonus kms and bail-out options

Because plans can change, we've included one or more options for extending or cutting short each running route. The bonus kms and bail-out options are described in detail at the beginning of each run, and you can find GPX files of each online.

Race routes

If you're like most people trail running in the Chamonix Mont Blanc region, you're likely interested in the local races, at the very least. Whatever your level—whether you're an experienced trail racer or a newcomer to the sport—knowing that you are treading the trails of an internationally renowned race route is a cool experience. For each chapter, we have included the names of the race routes that overlap with the featured run.

If you undertake all the runs in this guidebook, you will have completed parts of the following major races:

Les Contamines and Lower Chamonix Valley

- La Montagn'Hard
- La Montée du Nid d'Aigle
- Trail du Tour des Fiz
- Ultra-trail du Haut-Giffre
- Diagonale du Mont-Joly
- Chirv'Athlon

Upper Chamonix Valley

- Argentrail
- UTMB Mont-Blanc
- Marathon du Mont-Blanc
- Trail des Aiguilles Rouges

Valais

- Vertic'Alp
- Trail Verbier St-Bernard by UTMB
- SwissPeaks

Aosta

- Gran Trail Courmayeur
- Vertical Trail Courmayeur Mont Blanc
- Arrancabirra
- TORX
- La Thuile Trail

For complete details on each of these races, see the Run the Alps Race Finder, available via runthealps.com/races.

Mountain lifts and huts

Many of the runs or bail-out options described involve using a lift, and nearly all runs include stops at mountain huts. Keep in mind that opening schedules vary and do not perfectly sync up with the trail running season. In the spring and fall, always check lift and refuge opening schedules, so you know what food, shelter, and transport is available.

Getting there and back

There is a reliable network of public transport in the Mont Blanc region, and the runs in this book can all be accessed by public transport—although sometimes this will require more careful planning where the transport is not frequent, such as to Trient or the Col de la Forclaz in Switzerland. Train tickets can be bought with cash or a card at major stations, or on the train if you're leaving from a smaller station without a ticket office. Buses in the region can be paid for with cash. In Courmayeur, there is a bus office at Piazzale Monte Bianco. Guests in much of the region can make use of Carte d'Hôtes, issued by local tourism offices and distributed by hotels and Airbnb rentals. Public transport tends to be on time, but you may find yourself crammed in and having to stand for the duration of your journey. Timetables can be found online.

Hitchhiking is an accepted way to get around in the Alps. Many adventures don't start and end at the same trailhead, and some valleys are not well served by public transport, making hitchhiking a useful alternative. It's acceptable to ask others at the trailhead if you can ride with them, or to simply stick out your thumb! In the Chamonix valley, signs indicate preferred locations for hitchhikers to stand. If you are hitching, remember to stand somewhere with a space for the driver to pull over, and smile! We've found we get picked up more quickly if we take off our sunglasses and put on a friendly face. You can use a sign to show where you want to go, or just practice saying the name of the place you're trying to get to as well as another location nearby, in case you are misunderstood.

Hitchhiking is not without personal risks. Don't get in a vehicle if you don't feel safe. It's also prudent to know simple ways of defending yourself. When possible, hitchhike with a friend, favor daytime, and wear bright colors so drivers can see you. Please use good judgement and be cautious.

If things go wrong

If you or a member of your group gets injured or becomes severely ill and is unable to get down to safety, you may need the help of the emergency rescue services. In the Alps, this usually involves a helicopter.

Whom to call

Call the European Emergency number 112 from any run listed in this guide. Be ready to provide the following information when you call: name, phone number, location, altitude, number of people in the group, current weather, what happened, and what the injuries are.

Until help arrives

Keep the injured person and any other group members safe from further injury. Find a place away from hazards, such as rockfall, and sheltered from the wind. Put on extra layers of clothing and huddle together for warmth. Identify a large area (ideally 25 meters × 25 meters) nearby where the helicopter can land. The area should be free from obstacles, and you will need to secure loose objects such as trail vests, which will be blown about when the helicopter lands. When the helicopter approaches, kneel, and do not approach it until a rescuer tells you to.

Self-rescue tips

Luckily, most of the trails in this book are well-signed, and the routes contain bail-out options in case you need to cut your run short. If you have an accident but feel confident that you can get down to safety without help, it is still a good idea to contact a friend to let them know about your situation; if you are unsure whether you will be able to get out successfully, call 112 so rescuers know of your situation in case it worsens and you do require rescue. Before you set off, prepare yourself by carrying out any first aid required, having something to eat or drink, and putting on more clothing if necessary.

If you get lost, stop as soon as possible and take stock of your surroundings. Look carefully at a map and strictly follow what you see there, rather than what "feels right" to you. Remember that the map will not be wrong! The easiest solution may be to retrace your steps.

The values of the trail

What does it mean to be a great trail running citizen? That's a big question! To us, trail running citizenship includes being open, curious, respectful, and considerate with regard to our running community, other people, and our environment. We can apply all these concepts when out on the trails of the Mont Blanc region.

Part of being a good trail running citizen is understanding the place you are running in. The Mont Blanc region is the birthplace of mountain tourism, but while running is an ancient sport, trail runners are relative newcomers to the valley. Because of the growing popularity of the sport, most people won't be surprised to see you running on the trails. However, we think it's important to appreciate the long history of other activities in these mountains and try to understand how they have helped shape the culture of this region. It's also important to understand the forces currently acting on the region, including climate change and over-tourism, which are increasingly important issues in the area because of their impacts on the environment and tensions that may arise between visitors and locals.

As with anywhere you run, when you're in the Alps, follow the seven principles of Leave No Trace. Plan your trip, making sure that you have everything you need to travel safely in the mountains, especially for changing weather. Familiarize yourself with the route, with trail conditions and closures, and with local rules and regulations, which may differ from those you are used to at home. For example, swimming in alpine lakes is not encouraged and is even banned in some areas.

Be considerate of other users by limiting group size, keeping noise down, and stepping off the trail onto durable surfaces like rocks instead of moss when you are passing or being passed. Otherwise, always stay on the trail—even if other people don't. Dispose of waste properly: If you pack it in, pack it out. Recognize that as humans, we are visitors here. The true locals are the plants and animals that live here year-round. Be respectful of them by leaving what you find and being careful not to disturb or approach wildlife.

THE SEVEN PRINCIPLES OF LEAVE NO TRACE

1. Plan ahead and prepare
2. Travel and camp on durable surfaces
3. Dispose of waste properly
4. Leave what you find
5. Minimize campfire impacts
6. Respect wildlife
7. Be considerate of other visitors

Depending on the route you pick, there may be many other users on the trail. Because the area has so many international visitors, trail etiquette can seem a bit more fluid than you might be used to. Often, people simply yield to the person who is traveling more quickly, regardless of who is going up or down. However, this doesn't mean you should assume you have the right of way just because you're running. When you encounter other users on the trail, be a good ambassador for our sport. If you're coming up behind someone, announce your presence early to give them time to react. French is spoken on all sides of the Mont Blanc massif, so saying *Bonjour* is a pretty sure bet on any of these routes, but you can use *Buongiorno* on the Italian side. When passing, always say *Pardon* or *Excusez-moi* and never forget to say *Merci* in France and Switzerland, or *Grazie* in Italy.

Leave it better than you found it!

At Run the Alps, we try to limit our impact on the environment, but we also like to think about how we can leave a positive impact on the places we visit. Model best practice to those around you, and if you can, contribute to groups and organizations that are helping local communities and the environment.

UPPER CHAMONIX VALLEY AND VALLORCINE

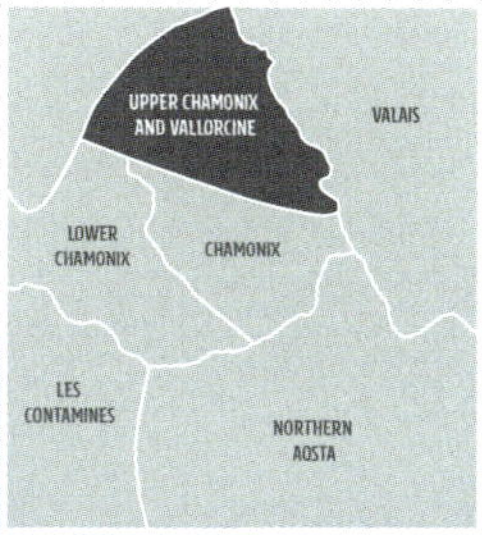
UPPER CHAMONIX AND VALLORCINE
VALAIS
LOWER CHAMONIX
CHAMONIX
LES CONTAMINES
NORTHERN AOSTA

1 LE PÉCLEREY

Across the Arve river and up through the woods on switchbacks with glacial views

STATISTICS

Distance 9km Ascent 687m Descent 687m High point 1984m

DIFFICULTY

1

TECHNICALITY

COUNTRY

WHEN CAN I RUN IT?

JAN | FEB | MAR | APR | MAY | **JUN** | **JUL** | **AUG** | **SEP** | **OCT** | NOV | DEC

STYLE

60% Forest Trail 40% Alpine

POPULARITY

ACCESS

Accessible by train and bus. Parking is available at the Montroc-Le Planet train station.

REFUELING

Visit the Ferme de Montroc shop to buy local farm products.

BAIL-OUT OPTIONS

Because this is a short loop, there is no bail-out option. Depending on where you are on the loop, either turn back or continue around.

RACES

Argentrail
Marathon du Mont-Blanc 90 km, 42 km, and 23 km

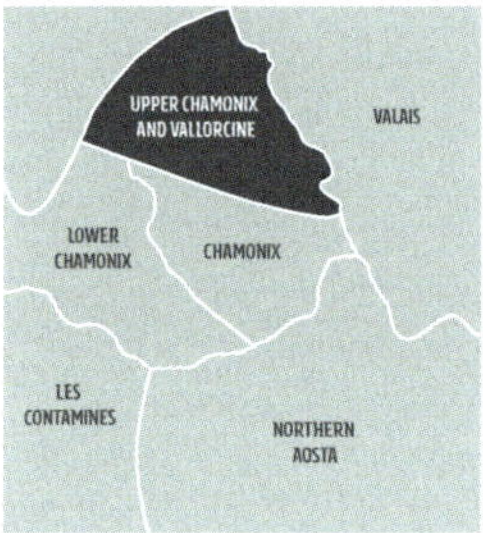
UPPER CHAMONIX AND VALLORCINE
VALAIS
LOWER CHAMONIX
CHAMONIX
LES CONTAMINES
NORTHERN AOSTA

PROFILE

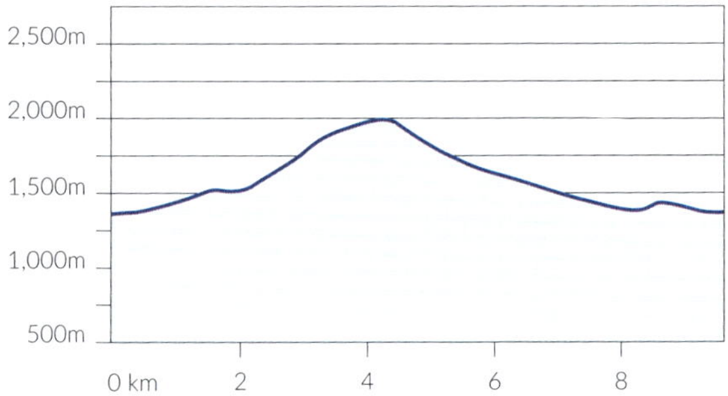
2,500m
2,000m
1,500m
1,000m
500m
0 km
2
4
6
8

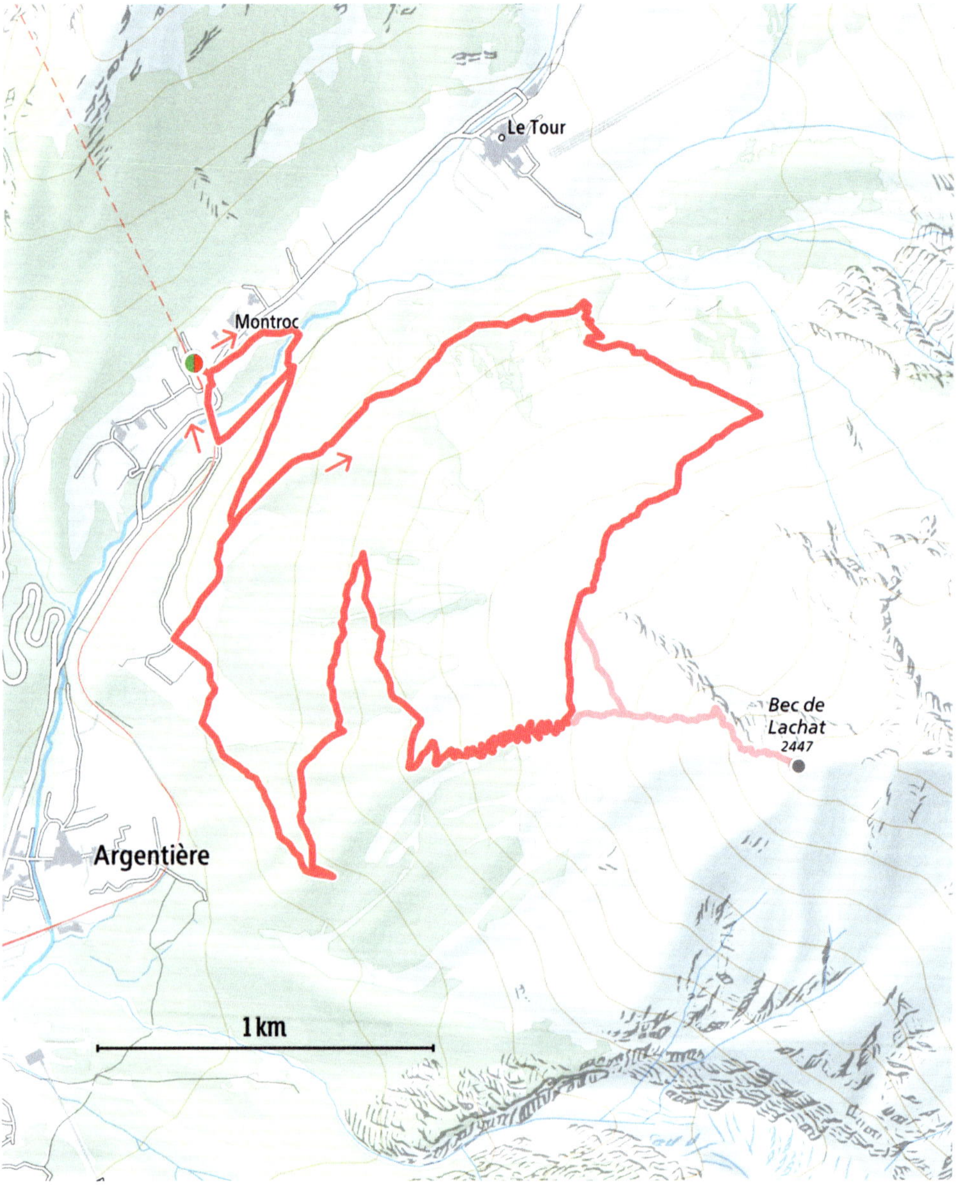
Le Tour
Montroc
Bec de Lachat
2447
Argentière
1 km

LET'S RUN!

Why we love it

If you have just a few hours, try this short loop, which has a little bit of everything: flowy forest paths, a few technical patches, big views, and a switchback descent that is sure to make you smile.

Getting started

From the train station, head uphill on Chemin de Paul À Ya, which was once the main road to Le Tour. After 100 meters, you'll come to a trough where you can fill up your flasks. Turn right at the sign for Sentier Piétons and cross the Arve river. Cross the forest road at the next junction and climb to the junction at the Le Planet pasture, where you'll have a great view of the old Belle Epoque hotel with Mont Blanc in the distance.

Péclerey

Turn uphill and then cruise toward Le Tour on a single-track forest trail, shifting down a gear and starting to fast-hike uphill at the junction, following signs for Le Péclerey. As you climb up switchbacks, you'll have excellent views of the Le Tour glacier. Several of the other runs featured in this book are visible from here, including the Aiguillette des Posettes, the run to Albert Premier, and Mont Buet. (See pages 24, 37, 49.) Snow can linger on the upper reaches of this run, so if you are heading off in late spring, consider bringing poles, and bring traction if temperatures are below freezing. The route tops out at an old shepherd's shelter, signed "Le Péclerey" and views open up towards much of the Chamonix valley.

Final stretch

And here's your reward! The route from this point on is a free-flowing downhill coast on an easy single-track trail. This big-air run might make you feel like you're about to go into low-earth orbit. Enjoy the switchbacks, turning left and then right at upcoming junctions, to finish the downhill at the Le Planet parking. Run up the field, stopping to say hello to Montroc's bovine residents, before rejoining the start of the route for a brief coast downhill; this time turn left and run the final few hundred meters past the Montroc farm, back to the single-lane bridge that will take you to the finish line. Fun, eh? We thought you'd like this run!

Bonus kms

Add 1.9 kilometers of distance and 442 meters of vertical gain, and you'll have your own, private Vertical Kilometer course to run. Follow the unmarked trail at the run's high point to a four-way junction, where you'll continue heading uphill. The route opens up as it stays close to the ridge, and you'll soon have impressive views over the Chamonix valley. On the final climb, this route curls to the right before reaching the summit of Bec de Lachat from the Chamonix side. With 360-degree views of the Argentière and Le Tour glaciers, Grand Montets, and Mont Blanc, it's a stunning vantage point. Run down the way you came, this time passing straight through the four-way junction to finish your run a short distance from where you started it.

Pro tip

Make a quick stop at the informal Ferme de Montroc shop a few meters from the finish. You'll be able to buy farm-made products including fresh free-range eggs and butter and tomme cheese made from the creamy milk of cows who graze on the rich grasses of Le Planet that you just passed a few moments ago!

2 L'AIGUILLETTE DES POSETTES AND CROIX DE FER

This run is a winner when it comes to views-for-effort

STATISTICS

Distance 14km | Ascent 959m | Descent 959m | High point 2199m

DIFFICULTY

2

TECHNICALITY

COUNTRY

WHEN CAN I RUN IT?

JAN | FEB | MAR | APR | MAY | **JUN** | **JUL** | **AUG** | **SEP** | **OCT** | NOV | DEC

STYLE

80% Alpine 20% Forest Trail

POPULARITY

ACCESS

Accessible by train via the Montroc-Le Planet train station and by bus via the Montroc train station. Parking is available at the Montroc-Le Planet train station.

REFUELING

Stop at Restaurant Alpage de Balme or Refuge du Col de Balme for some wonderful Savoyard cuisine.

BAIL-OUT OPTIONS

Turn right at 2.9 km, signed for "Col des Posettes" to connect with the descent route. Alternatively, turn right at the junction 4.8 kilometers into your run and follow signs for Le Tour.

RACES

Marathon du Mont-Blanc 90km, 42km, and 23km
UTMB Mont-Blanc MCC and OCC

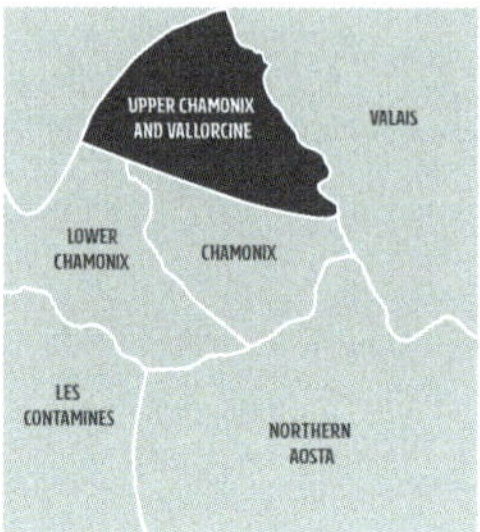
UPPER CHAMONIX AND VALLORCINE
VALAIS
LOWER CHAMONIX
CHAMONIX
LES CONTAMINES
NORTHERN AOSTA

PROFILE

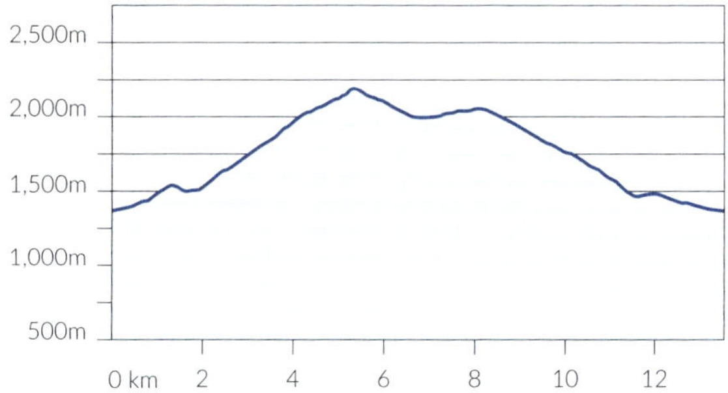
2,500m
2,000m
1,500m
1,000m
500m
0 km
2
4
6
8
10
12

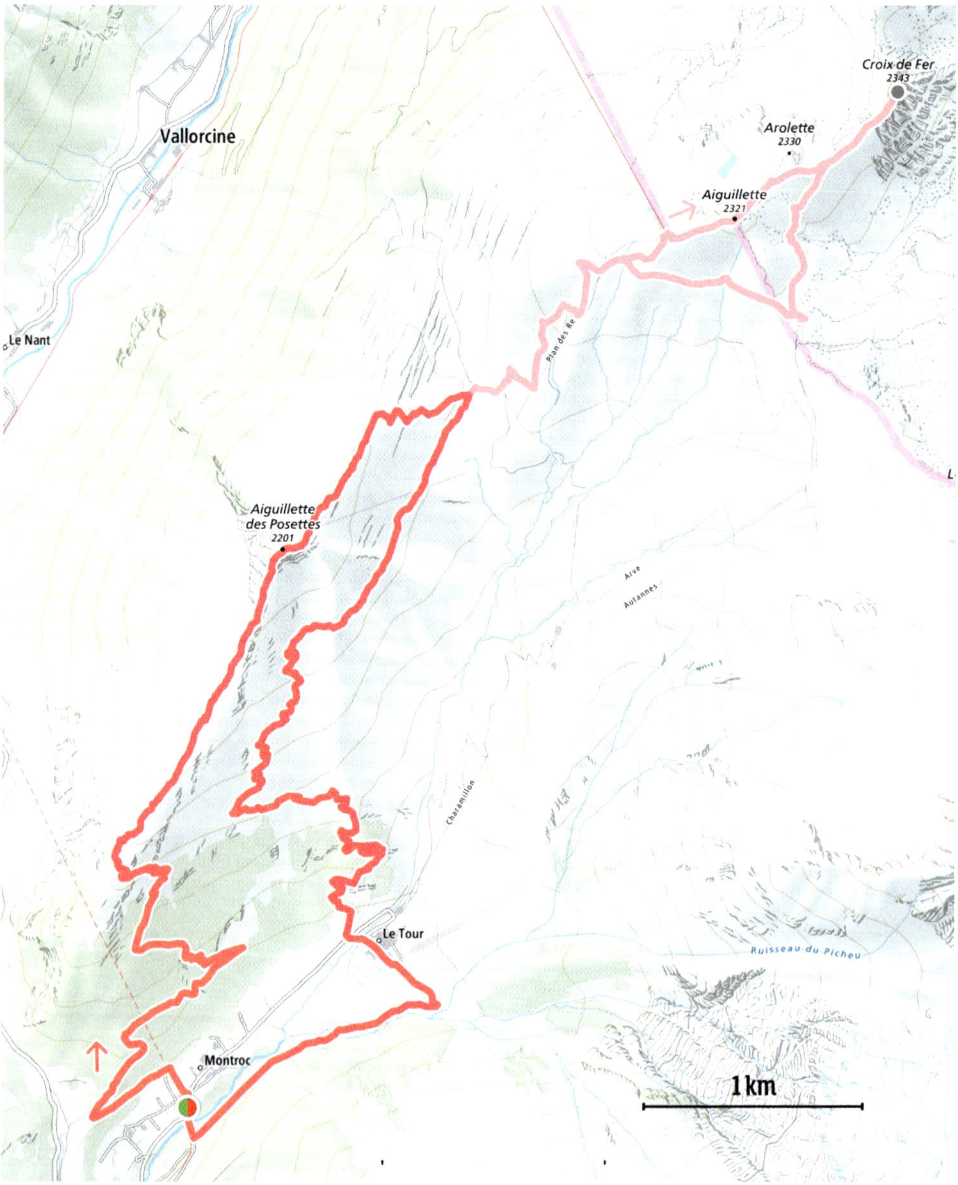
Croix de Fer
2343
Arolette
2330
Vallorcine
Aiguillette
2321
Le Nant
Plan des Re
Aiguillette des Posettes
2201
Arve
Autannes
Charamillon
Le Tour
Ruisseau du Picheu
Montroc
1 km

LET'S RUN!

Why we love it

This is one of the absolute classic trail runs in the region. You'll quickly gain expansive views as you climb the Aiguillette des Posettes—and they only get better! Add the optional loop to Croix de Fer to see a wide swath of the Swiss and French Alps. There's great food en route, too—so bring a few euros and save time for a culinary stop!

Getting started

Starting at the Montroc-Le Planet train station, head past the stone Belle Epoque Bel Alp residence, once a hotel, then over the tunnel and on to Tré-le-Champ. At the junction at Tré-le-Champ, double back and head uphill. Climb for a few hundred meters, turning right at the first junction. You'll pass the Chenavier Chalet, formerly the home of a Swiss dairy farmer who provided milk to Bel Alp back when these forests were pasture. Fill up your flasks at the reliable spring by the chalet.

Le Tour glacier viewpoints

Follow a gentle, rolling single-track trail to the next junction, then turn left. Climb tight switchbacks, entering the Aiguilles Rouges Natural Reserve. In a minute, a beautiful glen appears at a junction, where a covered spring provides another opportunity to fill up your flask. Continue ahead here, turning right in a few minutes at the next junction when you regain the main trail. You'll soon leave the trees behind, turning left at the next junction. A vantage point at 3.2 km provides striking views of the Le Tour Glacier and the Albert Premier Refuge. The trail on the moraine leading up to the refuge is Run #4 (See page 36.)

Summit of L'Aiguillette

From the ridge, you'll have panoramic views of Vallorcine and Le Buet, Mont Buet, Emosson Dam, and even the Dents-du-Midi range in the distance. If the summit is busy, follow the side trail for 100 meters to a cross and a bench with one of the best vistas in the region, plus some words of wisdom: *Quand tu arrives au sommet, continue de grimper* (when you arrive at the summit, keep climbing). Dance your way down a mix of technical terrain and pasture to Col des Posettes.

Le Tour village

Finish with a gentle climb, then cruise down the switchbacks to Le Tour. Run to the bottom of the Le Tour parking lot, then head through the old village on Chemin du Rocher Nay. At the road's end, continue on the trail, turning right after a few meters and finishing on a commuting route popular with the cows from the Montroc farm.

Bonus kms

These bonus kilometers offer big rewards, so plan to include them if time allows. Tête de Balme's grassy summit has 360-degree views, and standing on top of it, it's hard not to feel that all is right with the world. Croix de Fer has a fun ridge to run out and back on. Keep an eye out for undermined snow in the gullies along the way to the Refuge du Col de Balme in early summer. The run back to Col des Posettes is pure hero--running, as you'll roll through high-Alp pastures. In total, you'll be adding 8 kilometers of distance and 432 meters of vertical gain.

Pro tip

Both the Alpage de Balme and the Refuge du Col de Balme have great food, much of it locally sourced. At the Alpage, owners Michel and Cathy recommend their croûte au fromage made with local cheese and the homemade tarte aux myrtilles (blueberry tarts). The refuge in particular can get busy during Tour du Mont-Blanc season, so if you want to stop in, plan to arrive before 11 a.m. or after 3 p.m.

3 REFUGE DE LORIAZ AND LAC D'EMOSSON

Run high alpine pastures and finish in a classic Swiss village

STATISTICS

Distance 19km Ascent 970m Descent 1078m High point 2108m

DIFFICULTY

2

TECHNICALITY

COUNTRY

WHEN CAN I RUN IT?

JAN | FEB | MAR | APR | MAY | **JUN** | **JUL** | **AUG** | **SEP** | **OCT** | NOV | DEC

STYLE

60% Forest Trail 40% Alpine

POPULARITY

ACCESS

Accessible by train and bus. Parking is available at the Le Buet train station and at Parking du Buet.

REFUELING

Stop in at the Refuge de Loriaz for classic French Alpine hut cuisine or sample the diverse menu at the Restaurant du Barrage d'Emosson, which is part of the larger infrastructure at the dam.

BAIL-OUT OPTIONS

From Loriaz, return via the ascent route. At Emosson Dam, a steep descent leads to easier trails to Vallorcine. Public buses are available from TMR, and you can take the Vertic'Alp funicular-train-funicular combination from the far end of the dam.

RACES

Marathon du Mont-Blanc 90 km
Vertic'Alp

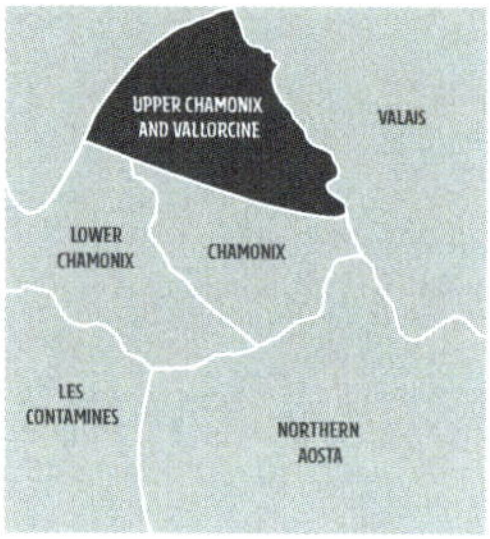
UPPER CHAMONIX AND VALLORCINE
VALAIS
LOWER CHAMONIX
CHAMONIX
LES CONTAMINES
NORTHERN AOSTA

PROFILE

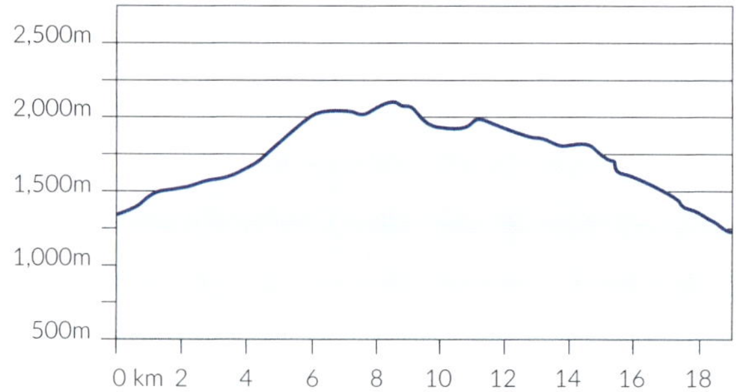
2,500m
2,000m
1,500m
1,000m
500m
0 km 2 4 6 8 10 12 14 16 18

Tête des Pelottes 1997
Lac d'Emosson
1920
140
Bel Oiseau 2631
Tête à Gay 2070
Finhaut
Finish
Route d'Emosson
Oeil de Boeuf 2652
Tête à Lugon 2373
Tête des Goilles 2351
Tête du Largey 2022
Sé Jeur 2062
Rte de la Forclaz
203
Giétroz
Aiguille du Van 2578
La Tête du Loup 1665
Le Châtelard VS
Le Perron
L'Ile
Carraye 2132
Pointe du Van 2278
Croix de Fer 2343
Arolette 2330
Vallorcine
Aiguillette 2321
Le Nant
Plan des Reines
Le Lay
Start
Le Buet
Aiguillette des Posettes 2201
1 km
Les Grandes Otanes 2680

LET'S RUN!

Why we love it

Vallorcine—the "valley of the bears"—is a favorite running destination of many at Run the Alps. It's quieter than Chamonix, with high pastures and big views. This run features no shortage of both of those things and is home to one of the best refuges around.

Getting started

From the parking lot, cross the road to run through the pastures and stone chalets of Poya. Check out the dramatic Cascade de Bérard, then continue running up the south bank of the river. Turn right to cross a bridge. Enjoy this sweet single-track trail and turn left at the Quatre Chalets spring junction.

Loriaz chalets

Follow switchbacks up through the forest, then continue through meadows to Loriaz. Little more than a mountain pasture for many years, Loriaz benefited from the arrival of the train line in the Vallorcine valley after World War I and the influx of tourists this brought to the area. But it wasn't enough—in the words of one farmer, Loriaz was "too high, too far, too cold." Today, Loriaz is home to an inviting refuge: with expansive views and great food, it's a great place to stop and refuel.

The hills are alive...

From Loriaz, traverse through alpine meadows, then descend toward the dam. You'll pass a series of large, metal avalanche-control tubes. The final section of this traverse is technical, with sections where chains and metal steps have been drilled into the rock.

Emosson Dam

Emosson opened in 1972 and is Switzerland's third-largest dam. Using underground tunnels, water is diverted from three sources, including La Fouly, a full 18 kilometers away. Cross the dam, taking time to admire Lac Emosson and the Trient, Le Tour, and Argentière glaciers.

106
B
B

Solitude awaits

Run down the road and take the trail on your left toward Fenestral. From here to Finhaut, you'll be on some of the quietest trails in the region. Coast down to the farm at Fenestral, then drop below the tree line. You'll alternate between steep, smooth trails and short sections of gravel road. Follow footpath signs at sharp turns, heading to the hamlet of Le They.

Final stretch

From Le They, continue downhill, watching carefully for yellow footpath signs. A series of switchbacks leads you down to Finhaut. Take the train from Finhaut to Vallorcine and change here for the train to Le Buet. Alternatively, run the final section from Vallorcine, following signs to Le Buet.

Bonus kms

From the junction with the dam perimeter road, run an out-and-back route on the road (or follow a combination of trails and road) to reach Cabane du Vieux-Emosson (see the pro tip below). Round trip, this adds 7 kilometers of distance and 325 meters vertical gain.

Pro tips

If you still want more, continue past the Cabane du Vieux-Emosson. Run the length of Lac du Vieux-Emosson until you arrive at the interpretive panels that give context to Switzerland's oldest vertebrate fossils, or "dinosaur footprints," as they are colloquially called. From there, return the way you came, or create a loop by descending through the Gorge de la Veudale. You will soon arrive back at the dam perimeter road.

4 REFUGE ALBERT PREMIER

Run a vertical kilometer up a glacial moraine to a famous alpine refuge, with the Le Tour glacier just over your shoulder

STATISTICS

Distance 11km | Ascent 1222m | Descent 1222m | High point 2707m

DIFFICULTY

2

TECHNICALITY

COUNTRY

WHEN CAN I RUN IT?

JAN FEB MAR APR MAY **JUN JUL AUG SEP** OCT NOV DEC

STYLE

90% Alpine 10% Forest Trail

POPULARITY

ACCESS

Accessible by bus and train. Parking is available at the Le Tour ski area parking lot.

REFUELING

Refuge Albert Premier serves a full menu—from snacks and drinks to substantial lunches with beer and wine. It's open from the end of May through the end of September.

BAIL-OUT OPTIONS

There are no convenient bail-out routes, but the run can be shortened by skipping the final 0.7 kilometer out-and-back jaunt to the hut. We don't recommend descending the steep moraine route.

RACES

None

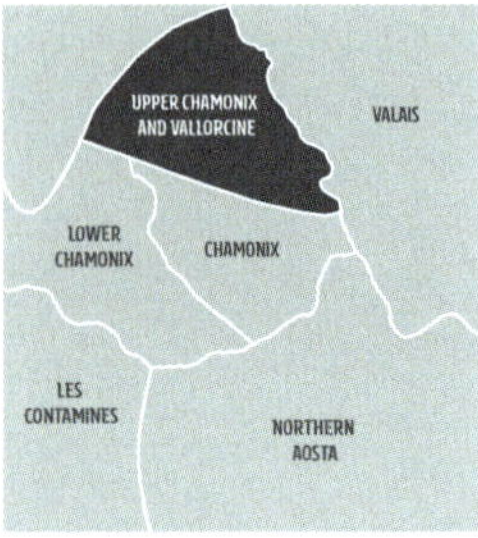
UPPER CHAMONIX AND VALLORCINE
VALAIS
LOWER CHAMONIX
CHAMONIX
LES CONTAMINES
NORTHERN AOSTA

PROFILE

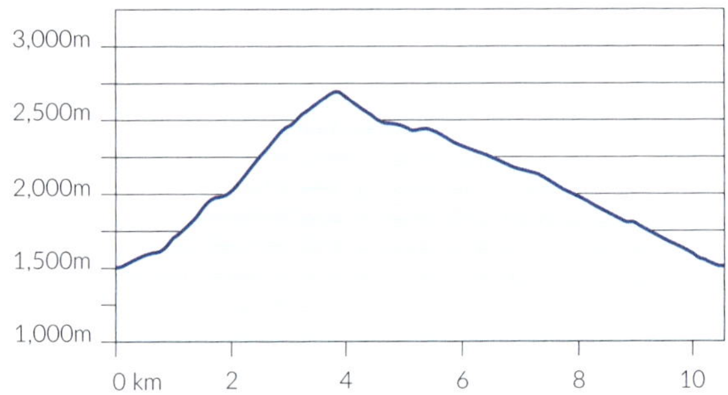
3,000m
2,500m
2,000m
1,500m
1,000m
0 km
2
4
6
8
10

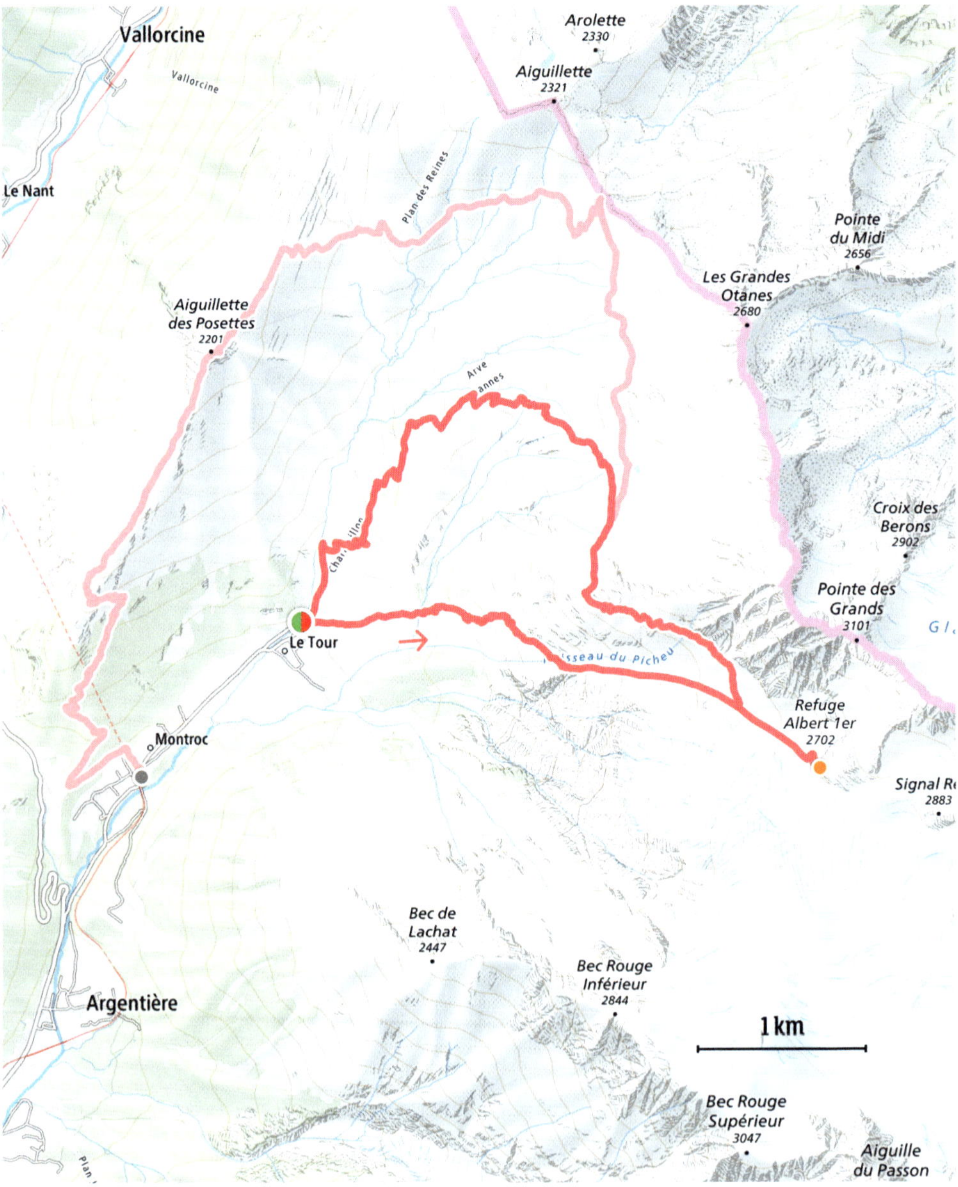
Vallorcine
Vallorcine
Arolette
2330
Aiguillette
2321
Le Nant
Plan des Reines
Pointe du Midi
2656
Les Grandes Otanes
2680
Aiguillette des Posettes
2201
Croix des Berons
2902
Pointe des Grands
3101
Le Tour
Refuge Albert 1er
2702
Montroc
Bec de Lachat
2447
Bec Rouge Inférieur
2844
1 km
Argentière
Bec Rouge Supérieur
3047
Aiguille du Passon

LET'S RUN!

Why we love it

This run features a vertical kilometer that sees you climb to the top of a glacial moraine and a famous alpine refuge. As you run, you'll be treated to epic views of the Le Tour glacier.

Getting started

Top up your water and make a bathroom pit stop at the bottom of the Charamillon lift before you head off! (Besides at the refuges, you won't find much potable water on this run.) There's plenty of vert to come, but the run starts with a gentle uphill on a faint track that crosses private pasture, passing next to and then under the Vormaine lift. A single-track trail leads to steep switchbacks. The views open up as you climb, with a few airy steps adding spice to the uphill push. After 2 kilometers of climbing, you'll gain an artificially constructed plateau. The building here is part of an extensive water collection system for the Emosson Dam, two valleys away in Switzerland. From here, water flows underground over 8 kilometers to the dam!

Up the moraine

Moraine time! Fast-hike—or slow-run if you are feeling ambitious—and wend your way up glacial gravel. Your destination is visible straight ahead, though you may find yourself distracted by the water crashing down to the valley in front of you and the occasional tumbling serac!

Albert Premier

After a final climb on technical terrain, you'll run past the old refuge to finish on the patio of the new building, where you can mix with hikers and climbers while enjoying one of the best views in the region.

Through Le Tour's high pastures

When it's time to head down, reverse your route to the first junction and take a right. High-elevation cruising with great views awaits, and there are cables and chains to aid in a few exposed spots. After some easy technical running, it's all single-track trail through pastures, past a herd of cows or two, and down through the Le Tour ski area.

Final stretch

If you like, take a time-out at the old alpage Les Ecuries de Charamillon. From here, head down through pastures and past the occasional flock of sheep. You'll finish right where you started.

Bonus kms

Like high pastures? Keep them coming by staying high at the second junction on your descent. Run to Refuge du Col de Balme, then combine this run with the Posettes route (see page 24). Alternatively, descend from the hut on the obvious trail to rejoin the route to Le Tour near the top of the Charamillon lift, adding just another 2.2 kilometers of distance and 23 meters of ascent.

Pro tips

Avoid the moraine if the weather is wet and consider an out-and-back of the descent route.

We recommend using poles for this route, and if you are doing it at the beginning of the season, check the trail conditions and carry microspikes.

When you reach the hut, grab a table on the patio for impressive views. If it's crowded, you can skip the bustle and enjoy a break 100 meters or so past the hut, where you can watch climbers cross the expansive Le Tour glacier as they set off to access routes in both France and Switzerland.

Looking for some fuel at the hut? You're in luck. Everything is homemade; notable favorites are brownies, banana breads, and a wildberry tart, which is made fresh daily. Our favorite lunch dishes include tartiflette and croûte au fromage. The hut warden, Paul, even makes his own foie gras!

For an end-of-run refueling, we recommend the ice cream at Givré or the formule du jour at Tête à Thé, both in Argentière.

5 COL DE SALENTON

A wild, remote, high-altitude run through nature reserves

STATISTICS

↔ Distance 25km ↑ Ascent 1473m ↓ Descent 2147m High point 2526m

DIFFICULTY

3

TECHNICALITY

COUNTRY

WHEN CAN I RUN IT?

JAN | FEB | MAR | APR | MAY | JUN | **JUL** | **AUG** | **SEP** | OCT | NOV | DEC

STYLE

90% Alpine 10% Forest Trail

POPULARITY

ACCESS

Accessible by bus. Parking is available at Parking du Brévent. This run is lift-assisted, so start by riding up the Planpraz gondola.

REFUELING

You will pass two refuges: Refuge Moëde Anterne and Refuge Pierre à Bérard. Both serve drinks, snacks, and simple hot food. They are open from June to September. Hôtel du Buet has a small restaurant that serves a range of hot dishes.

BAIL-OUT OPTIONS

There are no bail-out options for this route.

RACES

Trail des Aiguilles Rouges

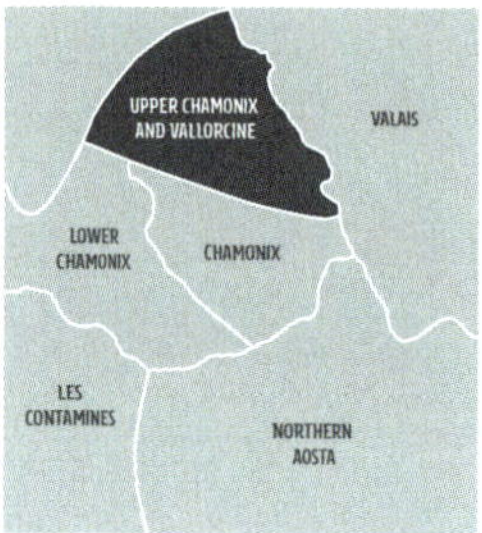
UPPER CHAMONIX AND VALLORCINE
VALAIS
LOWER CHAMONIX
CHAMONIX
LES CONTAMINES
NORTHERN AOSTA

PROFILE

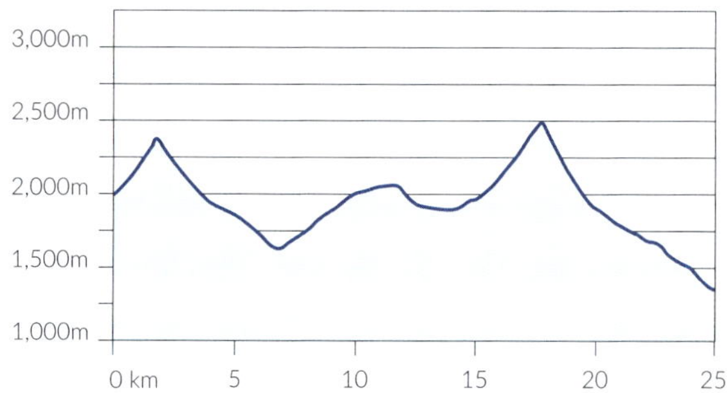
3,000m
2,500m
2,000m
1,500m
1,000m
0 km
5
10
15
20
25

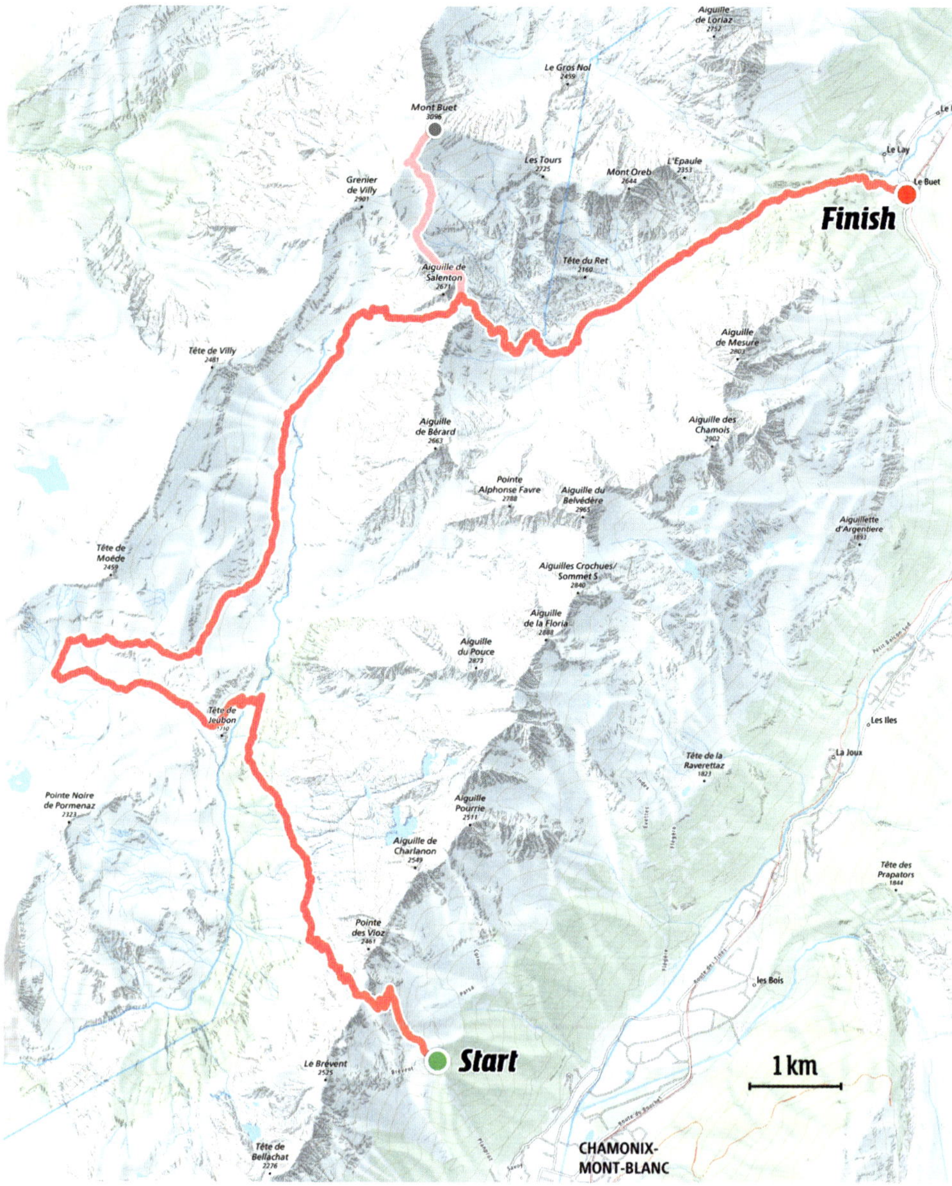
Aiguille de Loriaz 2752
Le Gros Nol 2459
Mont Buet 3096
Le Lay
Le Buet
Finish
Grenier de Villy 2901
Les Tours 2725
Mont Oreb 2644
L'Epaule 2353
Aiguille de Salenton 2671
Tête du Ret 2160
Tête de Villy 2481
Aiguille de Mesure 2803
Aiguille de Bérard 2663
Aiguille des Chamois 2902
Pointe Alphonse Favre 2788
Aiguille du Belvédère 2965
Aiguillette d'Argentiere
Tête de Moëde 2459
Aiguilles Crochues/ Sommet S 2840
Aiguille de la Floria 2888
Aiguille du Pouce 2873
Tête de Jeubon
Les Iles
La Joux
Tête de la Raverettaz 1823
Pointe Noire de Pormenaz 2323
Aiguille Pourrie 2511
Aiguille de Charlanon 2549
Tête des Prapators 1844
Pointe des Vioz 2461
les Bois
Start
1 km
Le Brévent 2525
Tête de Bellachat 2276
CHAMONIX-MONT-BLANC

LET'S RUN!

Why we love it

This entire route follows trails through nature reserves, so you're likely to see marmots, ibex, and even bearded vultures.

Getting started

From the gondola station, turn left up the wide gravel track. At the junction, take the smaller path up to the right, following signs for Col du Brévent. After 300 meters of ascent, you'll reach the Col du Brévent, which is marked by a cairn. You'll be able to see the Chaîne des Fiz ahead of you, and the start of the Dérochoir route from page 130.

Col du Brévent

Descend the rocky path into the Diosaz valley. The path is steep and technical for the first 300 meters but then becomes more runnable. Three kilometers of single-track trail bring you to the bottom of the valley. Cross several streams, then cross the Diosaz river via the footbridge and follow the path up the other side. The first 100 meters are steep, but the gradient eases off as you round the Tête de Jeubon. Follow the jeep track to the left and around to reach the refuge.

Refuge de Moëde Anterne

Head to the left of the building beside the refuge and follow signs to Col de Salenton. Keep your eyes peeled and you might just catch sight of a bearded vulture or two, which were recently reintroduced to the area. At Nants de Moëde (2014 meters) stay on the bigger, lower path. Before long, Mont Buet will become visible ahead (page 48). Continue up the path as it rises toward the col. The last part of the climb crosses a scree slope, then splits in two. Either path will take you to the top.

Col de Salenton

On the other side of the col, follow the indistinct path down to the left. There are often snow patches here, even as late as August. The route down is not always obvious, so pay attention to the route markers. After descending 300 meters, the path becomes more defined and will lead you right to Refuge de la Pierre à Bérard.

Final stretch

You can leave the refuge from either end of the terrace. After crossing a stream on a metal and concrete bridge, the path forks. Take the main trail, which ascends slightly to the left. Follow signs for Cascade de Bérard. When the trail emerges from the trees, you can run across the meadow to arrive at the Hotel du Buet. The train station is directly across the road.

Bonus kms

You can extend this run by making an out-and-back trip up Mont Buet. This adds 6 kilometers in distance and 500 meters of ascent.

Pro tips

Snow lingers on patches of this route until late into the summer season, so make sure to wear appropriate shoes and pay attention.

While you wait for your train home, treat yourself to a drink or meal at Hotel du Buet, which has been in the hands of the Chamel family for over 130 years and serves a range of delicious local specialties.

6 MONT BUET NORTH RIDGE

A dramatic, exposed run up to the Cheval Blanc and beyond that features plenty of above-tree line running and requires serious commitment from the get-go

STATISTICS

↔ Distance 24km ↑ Ascent 2044m ↓ Descent 2044m High point 3096m

DIFFICULTY

3

TECHNICALITY

COUNTRY

WHEN CAN I RUN IT?

JAN | FEB | MAR | APR | MAY | JUN | **JUL** | **AUG** | **SEP** | OCT | NOV | DEC

STYLE

80% Alpine 20% Forest Trail

POPULARITY

ACCESS

Accessible by train and bus. Parking is available at the SNCF Le Buet Station.

REFUELING

The Refuge de la Pierre à Bérard is open from early June to early September. A few picnic tables await at this simple but welcoming refuge, which serves drinks, snacks, and a small selection of warm dishes.

BAIL-OUT OPTIONS

There are no particularly easy ways to cut this route short. However, from Col des Corbeaux, you can reach Refuge de Loriaz, or, alternatively, you can head toward La Cabane du Vieux Emosson from the next junction.

RACES

Marathon du Mont-Blanc 90km

UPPER CHAMONIX AND VALLORCINE
VALAIS
LOWER CHAMONIX
CHAMONIX
LES CONTAMINES
NORTHERN AOSTA

PROFILE

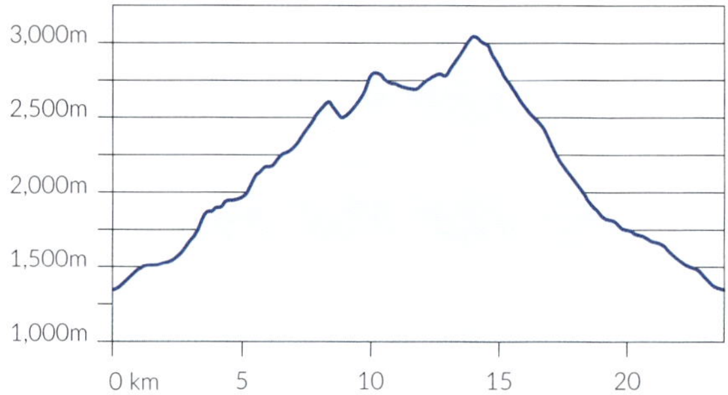

3,000m
2,500m
2,000m
1,500m
1,000m
0 km
5
10
15
20

Le Perron
Le Cheval Blanc (Sommet S.O.) 2800
Pointe à Corbeau 2686
Aiguille du Charmoz 2654
Pointe du Grenier 2775
La Cathédrale 2531
Pointe de la Terrasse 2734
La Villaz
Pointe du Génévrier 2870
Aiguille de Loriaz 2752
Vallorcine
Mont Buet 3096
Les Fonds
Le Nant
Le Lay
Mont Oreb 2644
Grenier de Villy 2901
Le Buet
Chalets d'Anterne
Tête de Villy 2481
Montroc
Les Frasserands
Aiguille du Belvédère 2965
Le Planet
Aiguillette d'Argentière 1883
Tête de Moede 2459
Aiguilles Crochues/ Sommet S 2840
Argentière
La Rosière
Aiguille du Pouce 2873
Tête de Jeubon 2686
Les Iles
Tête de la Ravèrettaz 1823
La Joux
Pointe Noire de Pormenaz 2323
Aiguille de Charlanon 2549
Le Lavancher
Les Tines
Aiguille à Bochard 2655
les Glières
les Bois
1 km
Le Brévent 2525
les Nants
CHAMONIX-

LET'S RUN!

Why we love it

Wild and dramatic, with 360-degree views that reach to distant corners of the Alps, this loop is not to be missed.

Getting started

The views start right from the parking lot! As you begin to run, you'll be able to see the North Ridge in the distance. Your route today shares a start with the Refuge de Loriaz and Lac d'Emosson run (see page 30); you'll run through La Poya and then head right to cross the Eau de Bérard river at 1.7 kilometers. After some sections of shady single-track trail, you'll reach Sur Le Rocher, your last reliable water source until the Pierre à Bérard refuge in 16 kilometers.

Up the Tré les Eaux

Fast-hike up the valley on rock slabs using the available cables. Next, head up the right-hand side of the valley to Col des Corbeaux. Mont Blanc will reveal itself as you climb.

Au Cheval!

From the Col, some above-tree line running leads to the classic climb up to the Cheval Blanc. You'll be well protected on the exposed sections, where you'll find ropes and chains. When you reach the summit of the Cheval Blanc, views abound, including of Switzerland's Grand Combin, the Matterhorn, nearby Buet, Mont Blanc, and the blue-green waters of Lac du Vieux Emosson at your feet.

The North Ridge and on to Buet

Rolling alpine terrain takes you toward the day's big event: Buet's North Ridge. You'll score dramatic views to the west after gaining the ridge. You'll want both hands free so you can make use of the cables along the exposed ridge. The Mont Buet summit is yours after a short final ridge run. You'll surprise hikers who took the standard route up!

Refuge de la Pierre à Bérard

Enjoy a ridge cruise followed by twisting and turning descending switchbacks. The trail becomes more technical as you get nearer the Refuge, which you'll first see from above, perched in front of the huge boulder that protects it from avalanches.

The home stretch

Run through the river valley and rejoin the ascending route at the bridge crossing. End your run with a beer at l'Hôtel du Buet, which has been operated by the Chamel family for over 130 years!

Bonus kms

Combine this run with the Col de Salenton route (see page 42) for a really big day out. After descending from Buet, swing right before Refuge de la Pierre à Bérard and run out to Plan-praz. You'll end the day with some pretty impressive stats: 35.6 kilometers of distance with 3096 meters of climbing!

Pro tips

- If you suffer from vertigo, this is not a route for you.
- Nearly all of today's run is exposed to weather and there are no easy bailouts. Be ready to turn around if necessary. Better yet, wait for a guaranteed primo weather day.
- Because of the risks associated with downclimbing exposed terrain, only head *up* the North Ridge.
- Bring poles if you like and can stow them. You'll want both hands free for the North Ridge.

CHAMONIX

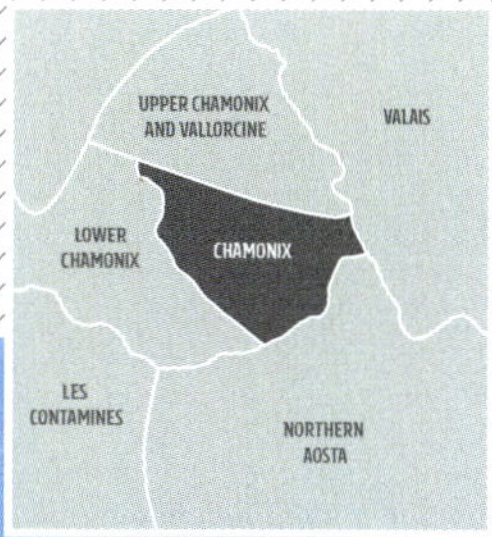
UPPER CHAMONIX AND VALLORCINE
VALAIS
LOWER CHAMONIX
CHAMONIX
LES CONTAMINES
NORTHERN AOSTA

7 MERLET

A shady forest run that loops around an animal park before following an easy riverside path back to Chamonix

STATISTICS

Distance 11km   Ascent 789m   Descent 799m   High point 1651m

DIFFICULTY

2

TECHNICALITY

COUNTRY

WHEN CAN I RUN IT?

JAN | FEB | MAR | APR | **MAY** | **JUN** | **JUL** | **AUG** | **SEP** | **OCT** | NOV | DEC

STYLE

90% Forest Trail   10% Road

POPULARITY

ACCESS

Accessible by bus and train. Parking is available at Lacs des Gaillands.

REFUELING

None

BAIL-OUT OPTIONS

To shorten the run, you can take one of the left-hand trails between Gaillands and the park that head down toward Les Bossons. At the park, follow the road down instead of continuing upward.

RACES

UTMB Mont-Blanc
Trail des Aiguilles Rouges

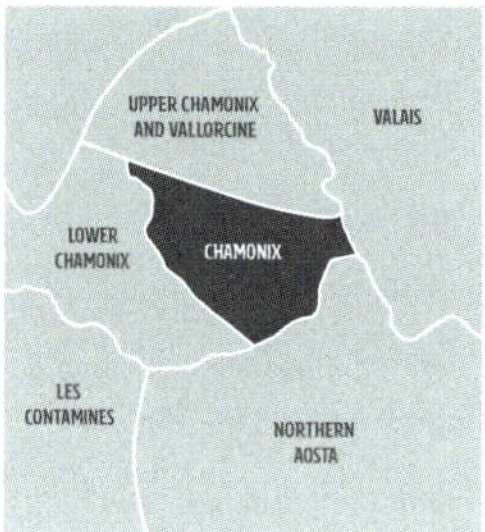
UPPER CHAMONIX AND VALLORCINE
VALAIS
LOWER CHAMONIX
CHAMONIX
LES CONTAMINES
NORTHERN AOSTA

PROFILE

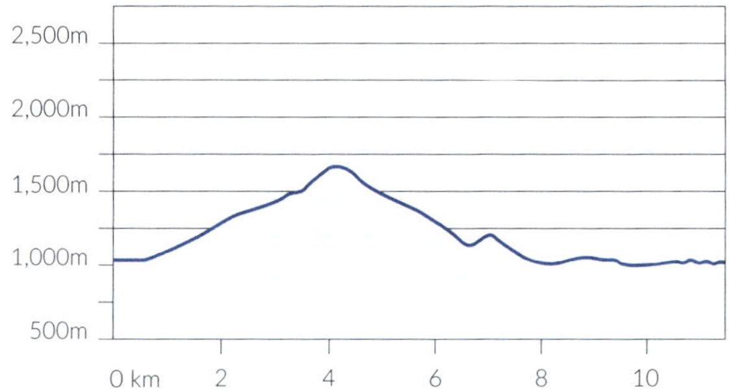
2,500m
2,000m
1,500m
1,000m
500m
0 km
2
4
6
8
10

Le Brévent
2525
les Nants
les Plans
CHAMONIX
MONT-BLA
Aiguillette des Houches
2285
Pointe de Lapaz
2313
L'Arve
Start
Les Bossons
Finish
Le Bettey
Les Granges
L'Arve
Taconnaz
La Griaz
Le Pont
Le Fouilly
Les Houches
L'Essert
L'Ormey
Les Gens
Mont Corbeau
2322
Le Petit Béchard
2150
Le Gros Béchard
2582
1 km
Mont Lachat
2115

LET'S RUN!

Why we love it

This route climbs up to Merlet Animal Park and then circles around it in the forest. It's a great choice on a rainy day because you're always sheltered. The nature-lovers among you will appreciate that you'll likely see some animals behind the fence. The trails are rough, which makes this a good route to practice technique on.

Getting started

From the Gaillands parking lot, follow the footpath for 500 meters in the direction of Les Bossons. You'll pass the climbing crag on your right and Lac des Gaillands on your left. At the junction, turn right to head uphill, following signs for the Petit Balcon Sud. After 100 vertical meters, you'll reach the balcony trail.

Merlet Animal Park

Turn left, following signs for Merlet, and run along the Petit Balcon, ignoring all side-trails. At around 3 kilometers, the trail becomes exposed. There are metal steps and handrails here to help you, should you need them. You'll cross a metal bridge before turning right and heading up the road. Just before the park entrance, turn right up some wooden steps, following signs for Chalets de Chailloux. You'll find yourself on the right-hand side of the park, where you can often see ibex through the fence. After 200 meters, turn left over a small wooden bridge, following signs for Statue du Christ-Roi. Continue straight at the next two forks, heading downhill, then take a sharp left turn. Just after the sharp turn, you'll enter a small clearing with great views of Mont Blanc and Mont Joly (page 144).

Statue du Christ-Roi

Turn right at the road, heading downhill and following signs for Statue du Christ-Roi. Just past the P3 parking, turn left down the footpath, still following signs for Statue du Christ-Roi. Follow this for about 900 meters, then turn right and right again. The "Christ the King" statue is 25 meters tall and made of reinforced concrete. Inside is a small chapel and a large bell, which can be heard from Les Houches. The statue was built in 1934 as an homage to Pope Pius XI, who was a keen mountaineer.

Final stretch

From the statue, head down the steep trail, following signs for Les Houches. At the road, keep descending until you come to a left turn, marked by a sign for Les Bossons. Follow this undulating river trail for about 2.8 kilometers, ignoring both side-trails. At around 11 kilometers, turn right to cross a bridge, and arrive in Les Bossons.

Bonus kms

Add an extra 2 kilometers and 100 meters of vertical gain by visiting Lac Noir. At around 5.2 kilometers, turn right to follow signs for the lake. At Plan de la Cry, turn left to start heading back down, following signs for Statue du Christ-Roi. For a longer extension, start and finish in Chamonix. Reach the Petit Balcon Sud via Chemin de la Pierre à Ruskin. This extension adds about 7 kilometers and 340 meters of vertical gain.

Pro tip

Do this first thing—before the park is open—to run on quiet trails. You're more likely to see the animals in the morning before it gets too hot. Make sure to bring enough water, as there are no fountains or rivers with rapidly flowing water en route.

8 LA JONCTION

A tough, technical out-and-back route to the junction of the Bossons and Taconnaz glaciers

STATISTICS

Distance 16km | Ascent 1636m | Descent 1636m | High point 2589m

DIFFICULTY

2

TECHNICALITY

COUNTRY

WHEN CAN I RUN IT?

JAN | FEB | MAR | APR | MAY | JUN | **JUL** | **AUG** | **SEP** | OCT | NOV | DEC

STYLE

90% Forest Trail

10% Alpine

POPULARITY

ACCESS

Accessible by bus and train. Parking is available at the Les Bossons train station or next to the Olympic ski jump.

REFUELING

Chalet du Glacier des Bossons is a small restaurant with a sunny terrace. It serves a range of lunch dishes and is open from mid-June to mid-September. Chalet des Pyramids is a small buvette that serves snacks and hot drinks and is open from mid-June to mid-September.

BAIL-OUT OPTIONS

This is an out-and-back route, so the only bail-out option is to head back down to Les Bossons. You can take the Télésiège (chairlift) between Chalet Glacier des Bossons and just above Les Bossons to cut out 400 meters of descent or ascent.

RACES

None

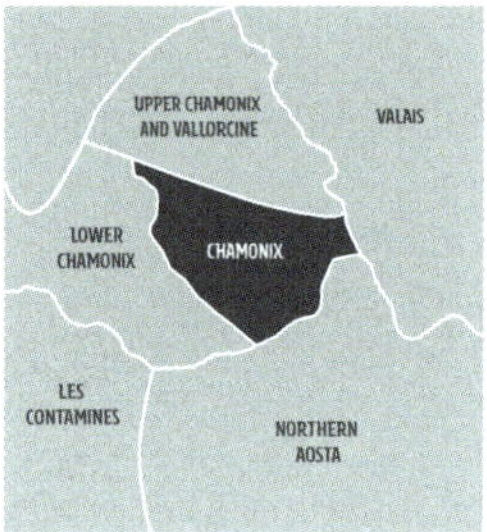
UPPER CHAMONIX AND VALLORCINE
VALAIS
LOWER CHAMONIX
CHAMONIX
LES CONTAMINES
NORTHERN AOSTA

PROFILE

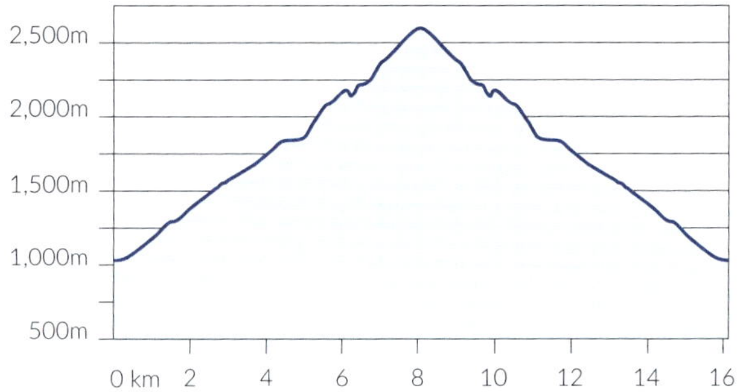
2,500m
2,000m
1,500m
1,000m
500m
0 km
2
4
6
8
10
12
14
16

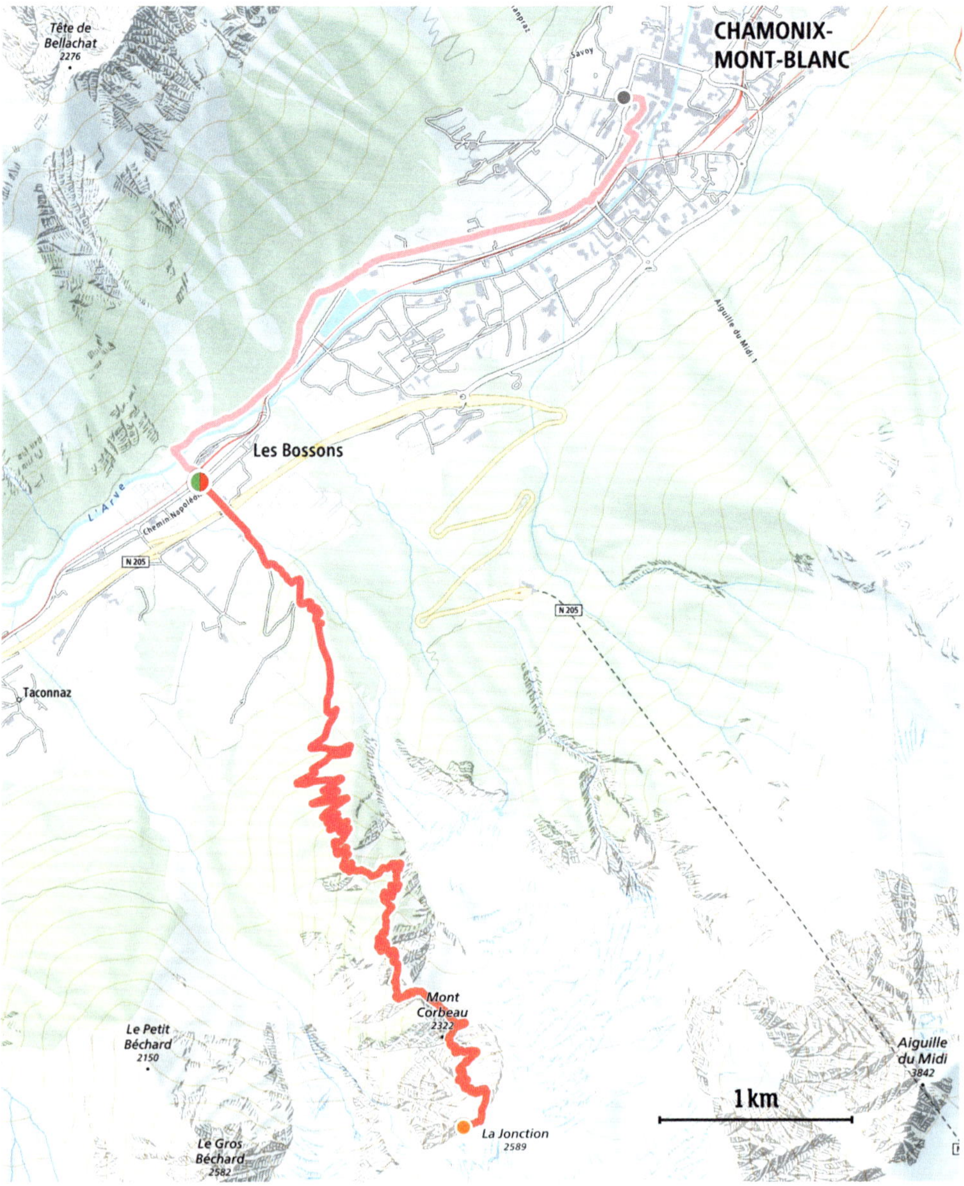
Tête de Bellachat
2276
CHAMONIX-MONT-BLANC
Savoy
Aiguille du Midi
Les Bossons
L'Arve
Chemin Napoléon
N 205
N 205
Taconnaz
Mont Corbeau
2322
Le Petit Béchard
2150
Aiguille du Midi
3842
1 km
La Jonction
2589
Le Gros Béchard
2582

LET'S RUN!

Why we love it

This route packs in a significant climb from the bottom of the Chamonix Valley up to La Jonction, where the Bossons and Taconnaz glaciers split. You'll get stunning close-up views of the glacier—the longest icefall in Europe—along most of the route before coming to a unique summit beside the granite "aiguilles" and creaking glaciers.

Getting started

Leave the Les Bossons train station by turning right onto the main road. After 50 meters, take a left, following signs for La Jonction, and turn uphill. Where the road forks, turn right to follow signs for Le Mont. You'll soon pass over a river—the Torrent des Bossons, which is the Bossons glacial meltwater.

Chalet du Glacier des Bossons

Continue on the same road, watching out for footpath signs to off-road shortcuts that will lead you up through the forest. Pass the small village of Le Mont, with its Olympic ski jump, constructed for the first-ever winter Olympics, held in Chamonix in 1924. Arrive at the Chalet du Glacier des Bossons for your first close-up view of the Bossons glacier. Follow a long section of switchbacks up through pine forest and then continue along an exposed section of trail with some fixed cables to reach the Chalet des Pyramides.

La Jonction

About 200 meters above the Chalet des Pyramides, you'll come out above the tree line, where the trail crosses over to the right side of the rough ridgeline. At around 2200 meters, the trail returns to the left side of the ridge. You'll reach a traversing grassy stretch of trail that will bring you closer to the glacier. After this, a sharp bend to the right leads to a steep rocky section, where painted blazes show the way. The gradient eases a little and you'll pass huge granite boulders on your way up to La Jonction. Although it may be tempting to scramble onto the glacier, resist the urge to clamber on the ice. It's dangerous to do so without the necessary mountaineering equipment.

Final stretch

Follow the same route back down to Les Bossons.

Bonus kms

Start and finish from Chamonix and run along the Promenade de l'Arve to add around 7 kilometers of easy running to the route.

Pro tip

On this run, you'll reach an altitude of 2589 meters on a north-facing slope, which means there's likely to be snow towards the top of the route early—or even late—in the summer. The highest section is steep, rocky, and exposed, so avoid it if there is snow. Fortunately, you'll be able to see the route from Chamonix to check for snow coverage before you head off.

9 PETITS BALCONS

A cruisy run up and down the Chamonix valley on gentle, shady balcony trails

STATISTICS

⟷ Distance 21km ↑ Ascent 711 ↓ Descent 711m High point 1298m

DIFFICULTY

1

TECHNICALITY

COUNTRY

WHEN CAN I RUN IT?

JAN	FEB	MAR	APR	MAY	JUN	JUL	AUG	SEP	OCT	NOV	DEC

STYLE

100% Forest Trail

POPULARITY

ACCESS

Accessible by bus and train from the Chamonix valley. Parking is available at Parking du Grépon.

REFUELING

Stop in at the Givré ice cream parlor or the L'Al'Pain bakery in Argentière.

BAIL-OUT OPTIONS

There are many side-trails turning off both of the Petits Balcons, which take you down to the closest village and are well signposted. All of the villages have a bus stop and a train station.

RACES

Argentrail
Marathon du Mont-Blanc 90km, 42km, 23km, 10km.

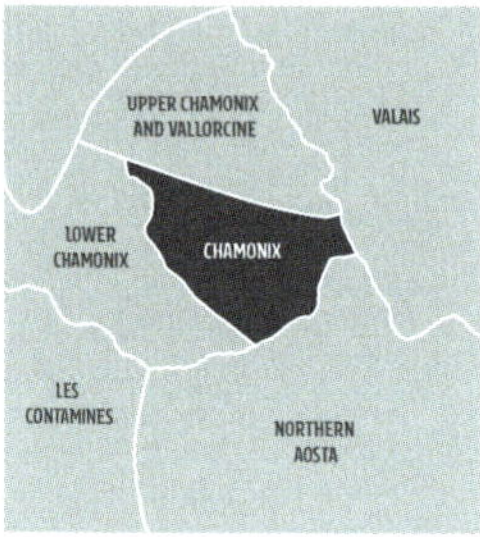
UPPER CHAMONIX AND VALLORCINE
VALAIS
LOWER CHAMONIX
CHAMONIX
LES CONTAMINES
NORTHERN AOSTA

PROFILE

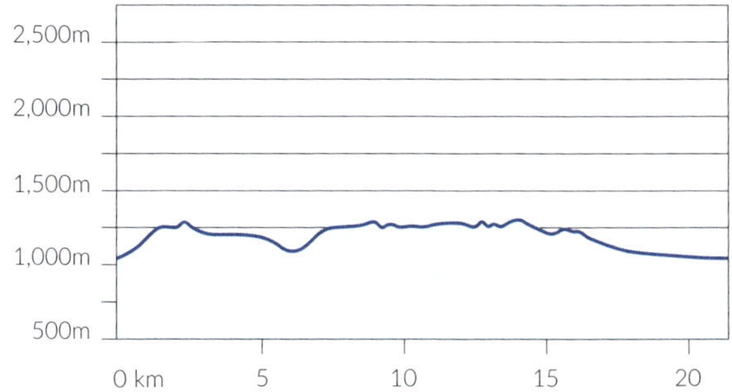
2,500m
2,000m
1,500m
1,000m
500m
0 km
5
10
15
20

Alphonse Favre
2788
Aiguille du Belvédère
2965
Aiguillette d'Argentiere
1893
Argentière
Aiguilles Crochues/ Sommet S
2840
Aiguille de la Floria
2888
Aiguille du Pouce
2873
Les Iles
La Joux
Tête de la Raverettaz
1823
Aiguille Pourrie
2511
Tête des Prapators
1844
Aiguille à Bochard
2655
les Bois
Route des Tines
Route du Bouchet
CHAMONIX-MONT-BLANC
1 km
Savoy
Plan Joran
Bochard
Index
Évettes
Flégère
Cornu
Parsa

LET'S RUN!

Why we love it

The Petits Balcons are cruisy balcony trails that traverse both sides of the Chamonix valley. Sitting roughly 200 meters above the valley floor, the balconies provide excellent vantage points from which to see the Mont Blanc massif and the Aiguilles Rouges. The route from the south-facing balcony to north-facing balcony is in shade for most of the morning.

Getting started

Start at Place de l'Église, Chamonix. Ascend the steps to the right of the church, then cross the road and head up to the Planpraz gondola station. To the left of the station, you'll see Chemin de la Pierre à Ruskin. Follow this and then turn left onto a smaller trail that leads into the forest.

Petit Balcon Sud

After 190 meters of climbing, you'll reach Petit Balcon Sud. Turn right to enjoy a fast stretch of undulating balcony trail. At around 4.8 kilometers, cross a ski run to stay on the balcony trail. Shortly after, the balcony will dip down to the valley floor, and you'll run along the river to Pont de la Corruaz. From there, continue up to La Joux and then Argentière. Head up the main street and then turn right onto Route du Village. Cross the Arve River and continue into the old town. Pass a water fountain and bear right toward the Protestant church.

Petit Balcon Nord

Pass through a tunnel and turn right toward La Croix de Lognan and Lavancher. Cross a wide wooden bridge and then enter a rounded tunnel. When you hit the road, turn left and then immediately right, following signs for Lavancher. Stay on this undulating trail, ignoring all side-trails. The path soon drops into a large clearing with a fantastic view of Mont Blanc. Follow the road through Lavancher and then turn left at the junction, heading uphill. Turn right onto Chemin de la Coutire and continue ascending until you reach the road. Turn left when you meet the road again and head uphill. Take the first path on the right, following signs for Les Bois and Chamonix.

Final stretch

At the road, continue straight on the footpath through the trees. Turn left at the road next to the helipad and follow it to Route du Bouchet. Cross the main road and then follow signs through the woods back to Chamonix.

Bonus kms

Add about 500 meters and 90 vertical meters by heading up to Chalet La Floria, a colorful stop with a big view and a variety of refueling options. To get there, at about 3.7 kilometers, bear left following the sign to the chalet.

Pro tips

The trail between Lavancher and Les Bois can be busy with large groups of bikers. To avoid these groups, set off early—preferably before 8 a.m.

Spoil yourself with an ice cream at Givré in Argentière. The milk is sourced from Montroc cows, and the shop features a unique list of flavors, including "hay" and "balsam"! We also recommend stopping at L'Al'Pain bakery at the bottom of Argentière for a buttery, flaky croissant or a crusty baguette.

10 GRAND BALCON SUD AND LAC BLANC

A classic run from the valley floor to a mountain lake, with clear views of the Mont Blanc massif

STATISTICS

↔ Distance 11km ↑ Ascent 1055m ↓ Descent 534m High point 2348m

DIFFICULTY

2

TECHNICALITY

COUNTRY

WHEN CAN I RUN IT?

JAN	FEB	MAR	APR	MAY	JUN	**JUL**	**AUG**	**SEP**	OCT	NOV	DEC

STYLE

90% Alpine 10% Forest Trail

POPULARITY

★ ★ ★

ACCESS

Accessible by train and bus. Parking is available at the Montroc-le-Planet train station. Descend by riding the Téléphérique de La Flégère (last descent is usually 5:00pm).

REFUELING

The restaurant at Refuge du Lac Blanc serves hot food and cold drinks; in the summer, the refuge operates a refreshment bar from 9:30 a.m. to 4:30 p.m.

BAIL-OUT OPTIONS

At Tête aux Vents, stay on Grand Balcon Sud to the Télécabine de la Flégère. This cuts out the final climb to Lac Blanc.

RACES

Marathon du Mont-Blanc 90 km
Trail des Aiguilles Rouges
UTMB
UTMB Mont-Blanc CCC

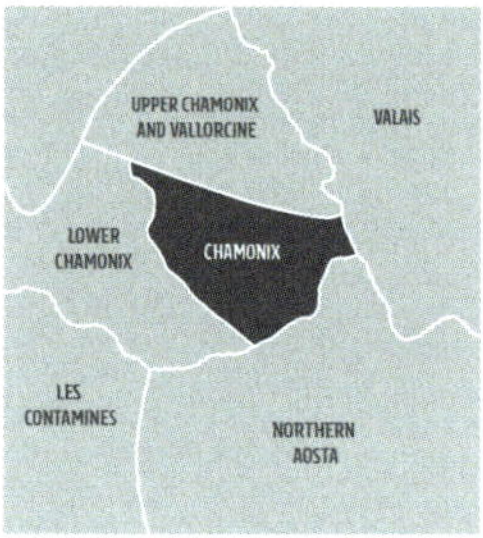
UPPER CHAMONIX AND VALLORCINE
VALAIS
LOWER CHAMONIX
CHAMONIX
LES CONTAMINES
NORTHERN AOSTA

PROFILE

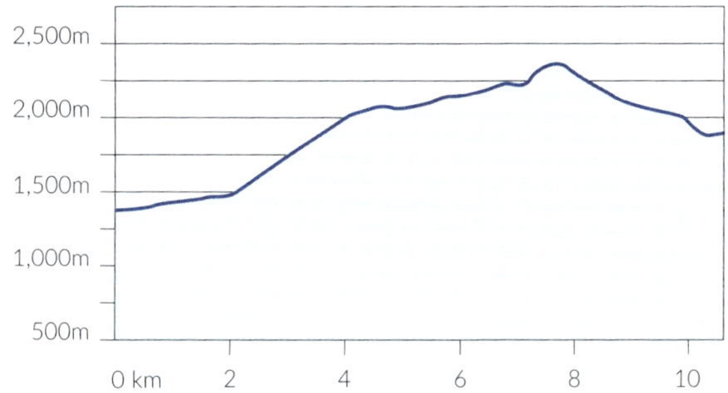
2,500m
2,000m
1,500m
1,000m
500m
0 km
2
4
6
8
10

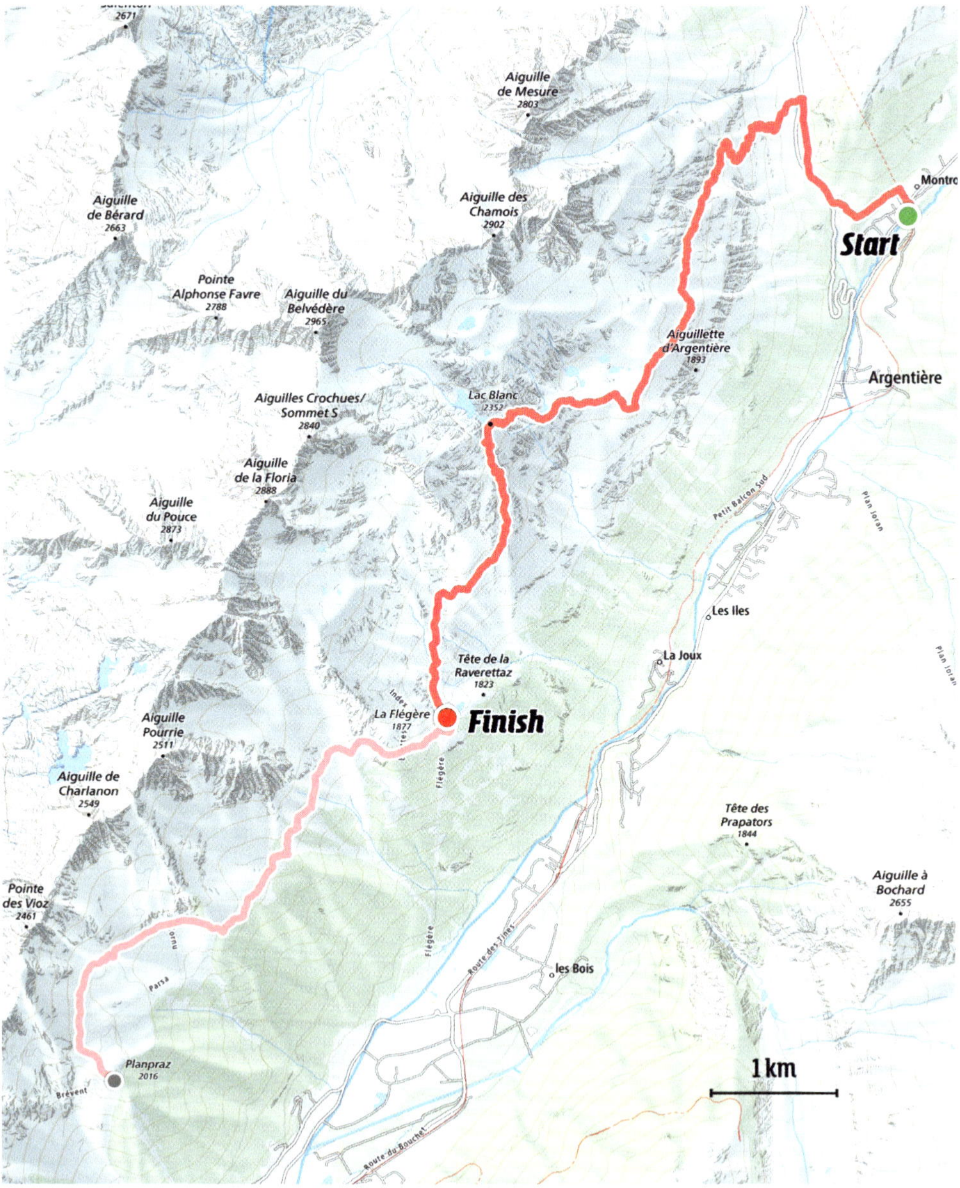
2671
Aiguille de Mesure
2803
Aiguille de Bérard
2663
Aiguille des Chamois
2902
Montroc
Start
Pointe Alphonse Favre
2788
Aiguille du Belvédère
2965
Aiguillette d'Argentière
1893
Argentière
Aiguilles Crochues/ Sommet S
2840
Lac Blanc
2352
Aiguille de la Floria
2888
Petit Balcon Sud
Plan Joran
Aiguille du Pouce
2873
Les Iles
La Joux
Tête de la Raverettaz
1823
La Flégère
1877
Finish
Aiguille Pourrie
2511
Aiguille de Charlanon
2549
Flégère
Tête des Prapators
1844
Aiguille à Bochard
2655
Pointe des Vioz
2461
Route des Tines
les Bois
Parsa
Planpraz
2016
Brévent
1 km
Route du Bouchet

LET'S RUN!

Why we love it

This is a classic run with unparalleled views of the Mont Blanc massif. It's also a great place to spot ibex, which often hang out near the trail.

Getting started

With the Montroc-le-Planet train station on your left, set off along the trail that crosses over the train tunnel. After 500 meters, turn right at the junction, passing by some totem poles and through a meadow. Turn right at the main road, picking up the trail on the right side of the road and following signs for Col des Montets. When you reach the parking lot at the height of land, cross the road to pass the Visitor Center. If you have time, take a look at the plants growing around the Center—you can find information about local flora and fauna inside. To the left of the Visitor Center, follow the trail uphill to Lac Blanc.

Col des Montets

The trail quickly steepens and begins a switchbacking climb up the ridge. There are staircases and ladders built into the path to help with your ascent. It is not uncommon to see ibex on or around this part of the trail, so keep your eyes peeled! After 600 meters of vertical gain, the route flattens and you'll find yourself running along a beautiful rocky meadowland. In the early summer, you'll often find patches of snow here.

Lacs des Chéserys and Lac Blanc

About 6 kilometers from the road, you'll pass a collection of tiny lakes called Lacs des Chéserys. One final uphill push with a ladder brings you to the hut at Lac Blanc. Lac Blanc is a classic outing, and with the Flégère gondola offering moderately easy access, you can expect to see other people here. The view is outstanding and there is food and drink available at the refuge. Stay and relax if the weather is good or take a tour around the lake—there is a second, larger lake further back. You've definitely earned a break, so enjoy it!

Final stretch

When you're ready to leave, follow the main trail down towards the Flégère gondola. The route down to Chamonix is steep and forested, so the gondola may come as a welcome option. It takes you down to Les Praz, where you can get a bus to Chamonix.

Bonus kms

Add an extra 5 kilometers and 200 meters of vertical gain by continuing along the Grand Balcon Sud to Planpraz, where you can get a gondola down.

Pro tips

Set off early to experience Lac Blanc with fewer people, and make sure to bring plenty of water, as there are no fountains on the route.

The quiche of the day at Refuge du Lac Blanc makes for an excellent lunch; the fillings vary depending on what's in season, but the dish's signature pastry crust remains consistently flaky. If you're in the mood for something sweet, you can't go wrong with the blueberry tart. Make sure to bring cash, as card payments are not accepted.

Asters, a local organization that manages the nature reserve, is working hard to reduce human impact on the area. Please stay on the main trails and avoid the temptation to swim in the lakes!

11 GRAND BALCON NORD

An adventurous run along technical trails that takes you above the trees and provides close-up views of the Mer de Glace glacier

STATISTICS

Distance 18km | Ascent 1347m | Descent 1337m | High point 2193m

DIFFICULTY

2

TECHNICALITY

COUNTRY

WHEN CAN I RUN IT?

JAN | FEB | MAR | APR | MAY | JUN | **JUL** | **AUG** | **SEP** | OCT | NOV | DEC

STYLE

60% Forest Trail

40% Alpine

POPULARITY

ACCESS

Accessible by bus and train. Parking is available at Parking du Grépon.

REFUELING

The Refuge du Plan de l'Aiguille, the Montenvers Café, and the family-run Chalet Buvette de Caillet all offer a place to rest and recharge with a meal, snack, and hot or cold drink.

BAIL-OUT OPTIONS

You can shorten this run by riding the Téléphérique de l'Aiguille du Midi up to Plan de l'Aiguille and taking the train down from Montenvers.

RACES

Marathon du Mont-Blanc 90 km, Duo Étoilé

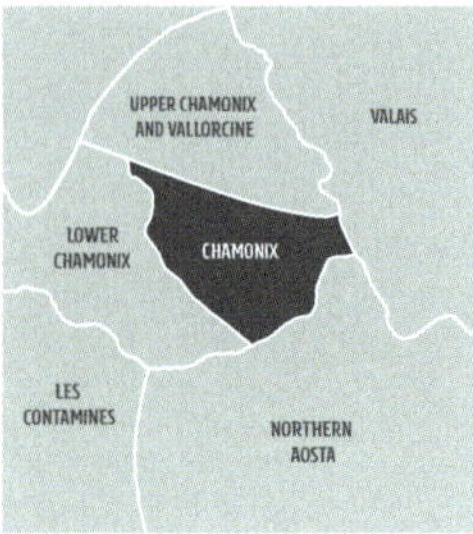
UPPER CHAMONIX AND VALLORCINE
VALAIS
LOWER CHAMONIX
CHAMONIX
LES CONTAMINES
NORTHERN AOSTA

PROFILE

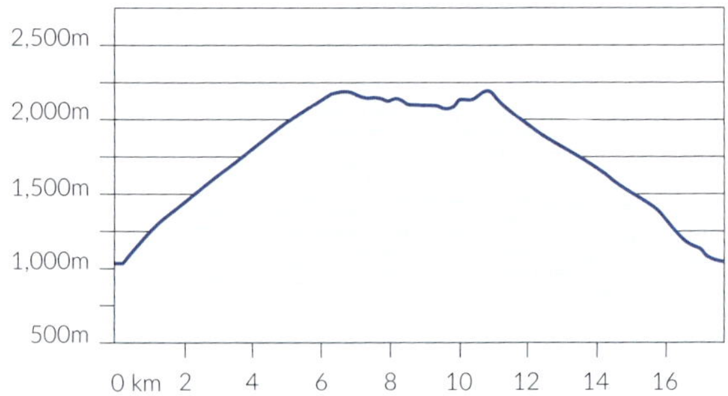
2,500m
2,000m
1,500m
1,000m
500m
0 km 2 4 6 8 10 12 14 16

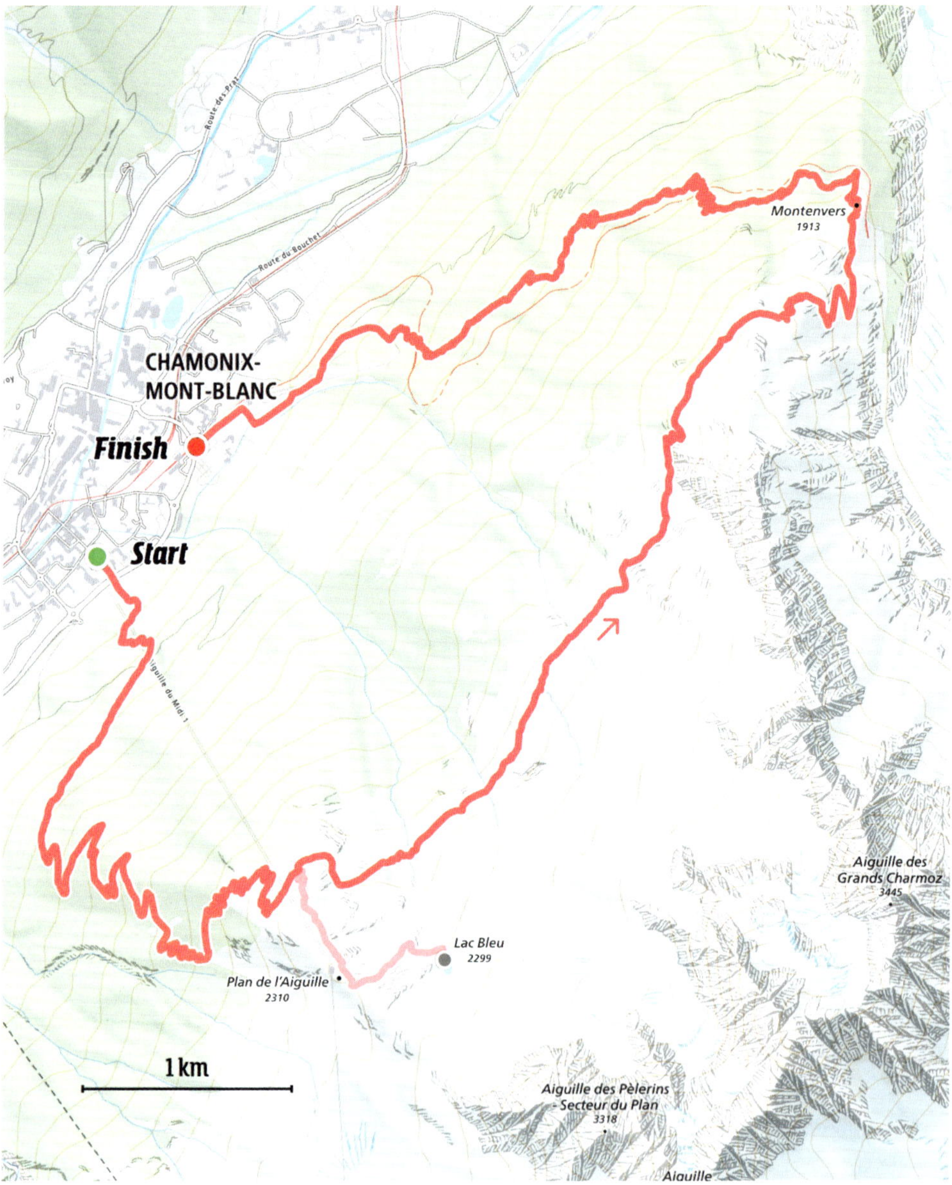
Route des Praz
Route du Bouchet
CHAMONIX-MONT-BLANC
Finish
Start
Montenvers
1913
Aiguille du Midi 1
Aiguille des Grands Charmoz
3445
Lac Bleu
2299
Plan de l'Aiguille
2310
1 km
Aiguille des Pèlerins - Secteur du Plan
3318
Aiguille

LET'S RUN!

Why we love it

This is a classic circuit with a beautiful high traverse. The route climbs up to the Refuge du Plan de l'Aiguille before crossing under the towering Chamonix "aiguilles," or needles. At Montenvers, you'll get a bird's-eye view of the Mer de Glace glacier, before finishing with a fast descent back to Chamonix.

Getting started

Start at the bottom of the Téléphérique de l'Aiguille du Midi. Take the small road that leads past the left side of the station and head through a tunnel in the Grépon parking lot. Continue straight across the parking lot to a footpath, signed Plan de l'Aiguille. The climb up to Refuge du Plan de l'Aiguille starts on steep zigzags through lush forest. At the junctions, follow signs for Plan de l'Aiguille and continue uphill.

Refuge Plan de l'Aiguille–Montenvers

As you ascend above the treeline, the path becomes rockier and you'll come into view of three of the Chamonix Aiguilles: Charmoz, Grépon, and Blaitière (from left to right). After 6 kilometers, you'll arrive at the refuge. From here, the trail leads you on a rolling traverse to Montenvers. You'll cross a few rocky sections and waterfalls. After 9 kilometers, the Grand Balcon forks—take the right-hand path to Le Signal, up several steep zigzags. At the top, you'll be able to see across the border into Switzerland, with a clear view of the distinctive Emosson dam (see page 30).

Le Signal Forbes

Follow the signs down to Montenvers and Mer de Glace. In just a few meters, you'll see the Le Refuge du Montenvers. This section is fairly technical, so stick to the main path as it bears right and follows the train tracks to Montenvers. You can get water right out of the faucet outside the Montenvers train station.

Montenvers and Le Caillet

This is the top of the train line from Chamonix, so you can take the train down if you want to avoid the descent. Alternatively, take the sharp right turn, following the trail down to Chamonix. Stay on the main track and turn left at all junctions, signed Le Caillet and Chamonix. At around 14 kilometers, you'll come to the little Chalet de Caillet Buvette, where you can stop for refreshments.

Final stretch

Continue down to Chamonix. These final trails are less steep and technical, allowing you to pick up the pace. You'll pop out onto the Planards ski run, which will take you down, at times alongside the Summer Luge and underneath the chairlift. Pass through a parking lot at the bottom of the run, then follow the road down to the base of the Montenvers train tracks.

Bonus kms

Add about 3 kilometers and 100 meters of vertical gain by visiting Lac Bleu, which sits just below the Blaitière glacier. From the Plan de l'Aiguille téléphérique station, take the main left-hand trail up through the rocks to the lake.

Pro tips

When the Montenvers cog railway was built, the Mer de Glace Glacier filled the valley up to the station. Today, access is a bit more difficult, but if you have time, take the new cable car to visit the ice cave, glacier, and the Glaciorium, a climate and glacier visitors center.

The croûte au fromage (crusty bread with cheese) at Refuge du Plan de l'Aiguille comes highly recommended.

12 AIGUILLETTE DES HOUCHES

A varied run on technical trails that peaks with an airy ridgeline jaunt opposite the Mont Blanc massif

STATISTICS

Distance 17km Ascent 1395m Descent 1395m High point 2285m

DIFFICULTY

3

TECHNICALITY

COUNTRY

WHEN CAN I RUN IT?

JAN | FEB | MAR | APR | MAY | **JUN** | **JUL** | **AUG** | **SEP** | OCT | NOV | DEC

STYLE

60% Alpine 40% Forest Trail

POPULARITY

ACCESS

Accessible by bus and train. Parking is available at Lac des Gaillands.

REFUELING

Chalets de Chailloux is a family-run buvette that serves hot and cold drinks and snacks. Refuge de Bellachat serves simple lunches and cakes. Both are open from June to September.

BAIL-OUT OPTIONS

Skip the descent by continuing to Brévent and getting the gondola down.

RACES

Marathon du Mont-Blanc 90km
Trail des Aiguilles Rouges

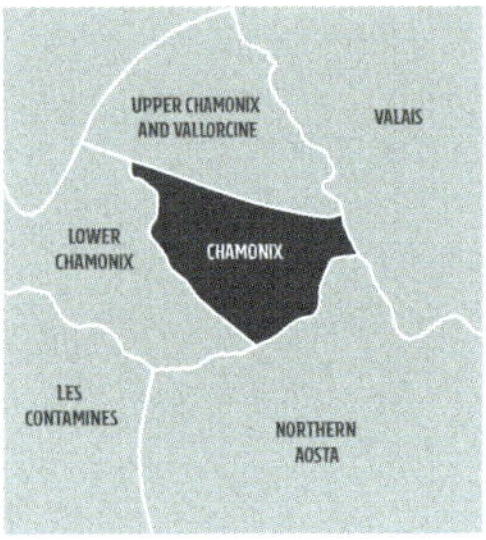
UPPER CHAMONIX AND VALLORCINE
VALAIS
LOWER CHAMONIX
CHAMONIX
LES CONTAMINES
NORTHERN AOSTA

PROFILE

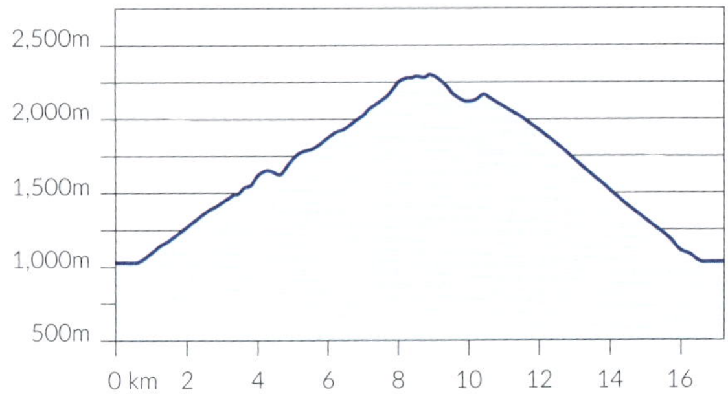
2,500m
2,000m
1,500m
1,000m
500m
0 km
2
4
6
8
10
12
14
16

Le Brévent
2525
Brévent
Parsa
Planpraz
Savoy
Tête de Bellachat
2276
Aiguillette des Houches
2285
Pointe de Lapaz
2313
Les Bossons
L'Arve
Chemin Napoléon
N 205
N 205
Taconnaz
Le Pont
Les Houches
1 km

LET'S RUN!

Why we love it

Aiguillette des Houches is a 2000-meter peak that sits directly opposite the north face of Mont Blanc. Running along the ridgeline, you'll get the classic view of this local giant, followed by vistas of the tumbling Les Bossons glacier and the dark, rocky Aiguilles de Chamonix. The trails on this route are technical without being too remote.

Getting started

From the Gaillands parking lot, follow the footpath toward Les Bossons for 500 meters. You'll pass the climbing wall on your right and Lac des Gaillands on your left. At the junction, turn right to head uphill, following signs for the Petit Balcon Sud. After 100 vertical meters, you'll reach the balcony trail.

Chalets de Chailloux

Turn left, following signs for Merlet, and run along the Petit Balcon Sud for about 2.5 kilometers, ignoring all side-trails. Turn right at the road and head towards the Merlet Animal Park. Turn right up a set of wooden steps just before the park entrance, following signs for Chalets de Chailloux. After 200 meters, turn left over a small wooden bridge. Turn right at the next junction, heading uphill towards Chalets de Chailloux. Continue up this wide track as it zigzags up the slope. You'll soon emerge from the trees to fantastic views of the Mont Blanc massif.

Aiguillette des Houches

At the chalets, take the trail on your right, following signs for Aiguillette des Houches. This path soon becomes uneven, and the final climb is rocky. From the top, you'll have a clear view of the Mont Blanc massif in one direction and the Chaîne des Fiz in the other. Bear right to follow the unmarked trail along the ridge. The path starts out grassy and then becomes rocky. Partway along—around 9.5 kilometers in—the path forks, and you have the option of heading either left or right around the ridge. Go left if you prefer a less technical trail (which is the route our map follows). At around 10 kilometers, turn left to follow the overgrown path through shrubs. Follow this trail as it continues around a small lake and then leads to the refuge.

Final stretch

From the refuge, it's time for a classic descent back down to Lac des Gaillands. Descend the wide avalanche gully on steep, rocky switchbacks for about 2 kilometers. You'll gradually come under the cover of trees, where the trail will become more runnable. As you cruise down the forest path, follow signs for Chamonix and Gaillands.

Bonus kms

Add 2 kilometers by starting and finishing in the center of Chamonix.

Pro tips

There are no fountains on this route, so make sure to bring enough water with you.

Try a selection of local cheeses and meats with bread at Chalets de Chailloux to refuel with a traditional mountain snack.

LOWER CHAMONIX VALLEY

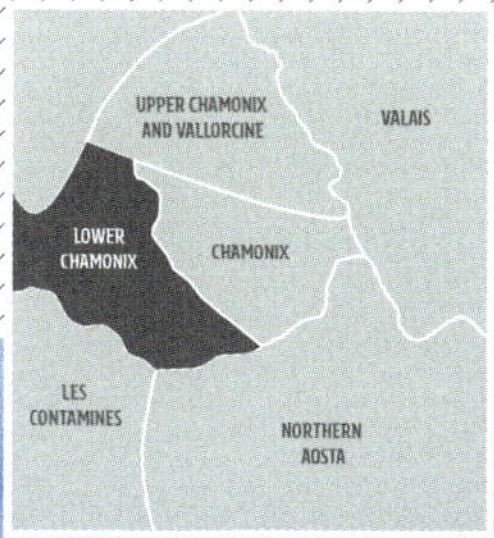

UPPER CHAMONIX AND VALLORCINE
VALAIS
LOWER CHAMONIX
CHAMONIX
LES CONTAMINES
NORTHERN AOSTA

13 BIONNASSAY AND SUSPENSION BRIDGE

Use the Bellevue cable car to get up high fast, then run through a quaint village and over a suspension bridge beneath glaciers

STATISTICS

Distance 9km Ascent 582 Descent 582m High point 1801m

DIFFICULTY

1

TECHNICALITY

COUNTRY

WHEN CAN I RUN IT?

JAN FEB MAR APR MAY **JUN JUL AUG SEP** OCT NOV DEC

STYLE

80% Forest Trail 10% Road 10% Alpine

POPULARITY

ACCESS

Accessible by bus and train (the request stop Viaduc St. Marie train station is 1.2 kilometers from the lift station). Parking is available at Parking de Bellevue Les Houches. Start by riding the Télécabine du Bellevue.

REFUELING

The Chalette snack bar at the top of the Bellevue is open when the cable car is open and serves small lunches and ice cream.

BAIL-OUT OPTIONS

From Bionnassay, walk down the road to Bionnay, where you can get the bus that runs regularly from Les Contamines to Le Fayet. From Le Fayet, you can get a train to the Chamonix valley.

RACES

La Montée du Nid d'Aigle
UTMB Mont-Blanc TDS

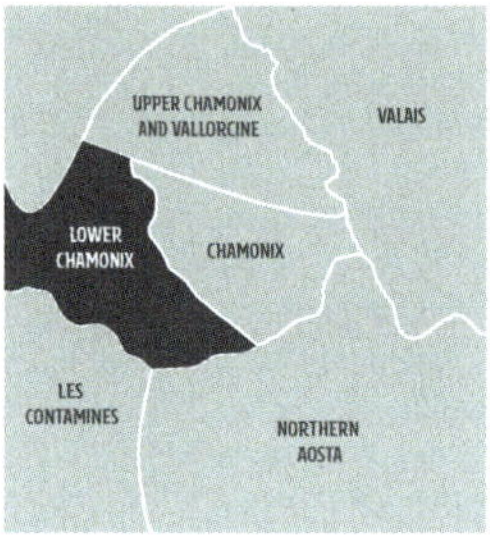
UPPER CHAMONIX AND VALLORCINE
VALAIS
LOWER CHAMONIX
CHAMONIX
LES CONTAMINES
NORTHERN AOSTA

PROFILE

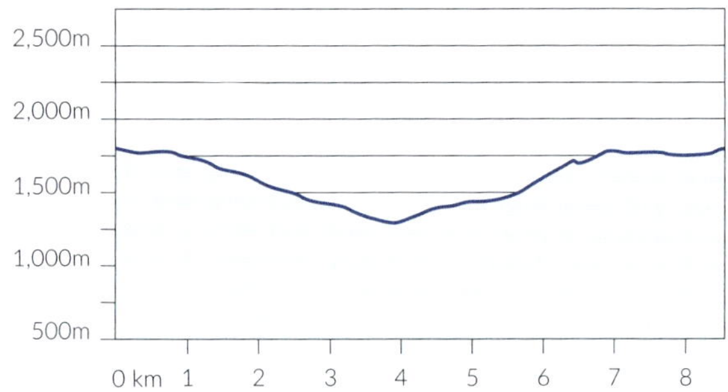
2,500m
2,000m
1,500m
1,000m
500m
0 km
1
2
3
4
5
6
7
8

Tête de la Charme
1870
Kandahar
Voza-Prarion
Bellevue
1801
Bionnassay
Mont Vorassay
2299
Col de Tricot
2021
1 km

LET'S RUN!

Why we love it

This run starts with a tram ride up to the Bellevue summit at 1801 meters, where the air is cooler and the views are bigger. It's called Bellevue—"beautiful view"—for a reason! From there, it follows the famous Tour du Mont-Blanc route, which crosses a long suspension bridge, or "passerelle," beneath the Bionnassay glacier. This is a gentle run that makes the most of being up high.

Getting started

Ride the tram up to Bellevue, then take the jeep track down to the right, following signs for Col de Voza. In the winter, this slope is a beginner ski run! You'll cross the Mont Blanc tramway tracks and arrive at Col de Voza station. Take the jeep track on the left down to Bionnassay. The jeep track soon becomes a road, and you'll follow it past the Le Crozat parking lot. Continue down the road to the village of Bionnassay.

Bionnassay

Just before a large water trough, turn left off the road, following signs for Le Champel. Descend past the Bionnassay chapel, then join a single-track trail to cross the Bionnassay river via a footbridge. Once across the bridge, a steep climb brings you to a junction at L'Ormey, where you'll turn left onto the jeep track, following signs for Passerelle du Glacier.

Passerelle du Glacier

A gentle ascent brings you to Chalère, where you'll turn right into the forest. After a steep, shady climb, you'll arrive at a junction and the Tour du Mont Blanc variant route. Turn left here, following signs for Bellevue, and descend a rocky trail. Cross the suspension bridge over the turbulent meltwaters of the Bionnassay glacier and then follow the trail up the other side, ascending the old glacial moraine. These high rocky ridges were formed when the glacier scoured its path hundreds of years ago.

Final stretch

When you reach a meadow, bear left to traverse the hillside. There are a couple of rocky sections with handrails to hold if you need them. Turn right up a short, steep ascent, then cross the tramline and return to the Bellevue gondola station.

AUBERGE
DE
BIONNASSAY

Auberge
de Bionnassay

ANNE
haute savoie

Bonus kms

You can add an extra 300 meters of ascent and 5 kilometers of distance by extending this route with an out-and-back run to the Col de Tricot at 2120 meters. Take the path up to the right at the junction just before the Passerelle.

Pro tips

The Bellevue cable car is open every day from mid-June until mid-September (check online for the exact dates). If it isn't open, you can go up on foot. Follow the signed Tour du Mont-Blanc route up to the Col de Voza and continue the run from there.

Restaurant La Chalette serves homemade pastries, ice cream and sorbets.

14 TÊTE DE LA CHARME

A gentle, lift-assisted run that starts above 1800 meters elevation and circles around a grassy peak on well-marked trails

STATISTICS

⟷ Distance 7km ↑ Ascent 316m ↓ Descent 316m High point 1969m

DIFFICULTY

1

TECHNICALITY

COUNTRY

WHEN CAN I RUN IT?

JAN	FEB	MAR	APR	MAY	JUN	JUL	AUG	SEP	OCT	NOV	DEC

STYLE

90% Alpine 10% Forest Trail

POPULARITY

ACCESS

Accessible by bus and train (the Viaduc St. Marie request train stop is 0.7 kilometers from the lift station). Parking is available at Parking du Prarion. Start by riding the Télécabine du Prarion.

REFUELING

At around 3.5 kilometers, make a small detour by turning left down a grassy path to Restaurant La Cha. Alternatively, at the end of your run, enjoy a refreshment on the terrace at Hôtel Le Prarion.

BAIL-OUT OPTIONS

At 4.5 kilometers, instead of turning left up to the Le Prarion summit, continue straight, following signs for Hôtel Le Prarion. Take the left path to the side of the hotel and then head down to the Prarion gondola.

RACES

None

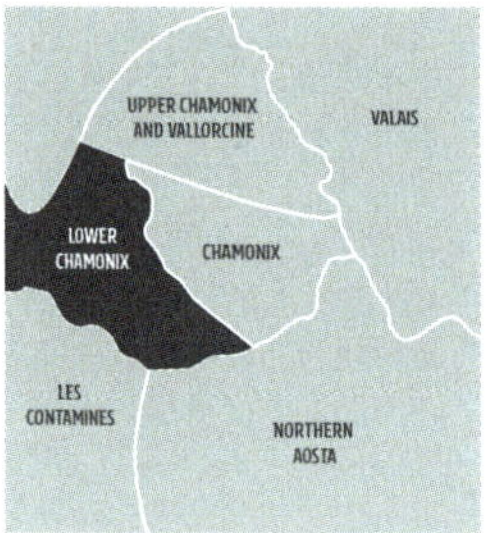
UPPER CHAMONIX AND VALLORCINE
VALAIS
LOWER CHAMONIX
CHAMONIX
LES CONTAMINES
NORTHERN AOSTA

PROFILE

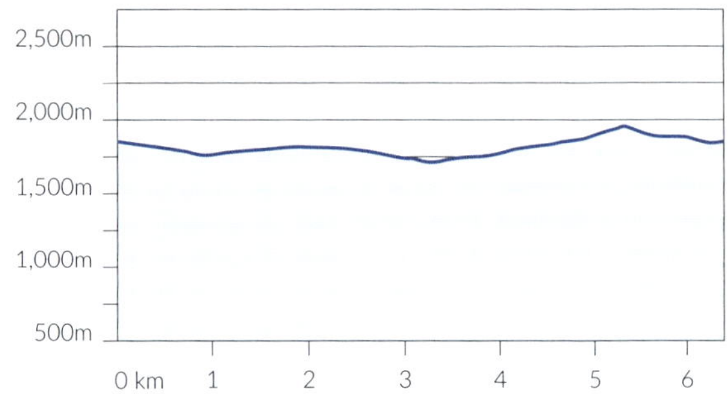
2,500m
2,000m
1,500m
1,000m
500m
0 km
1
2
3
4
5
6

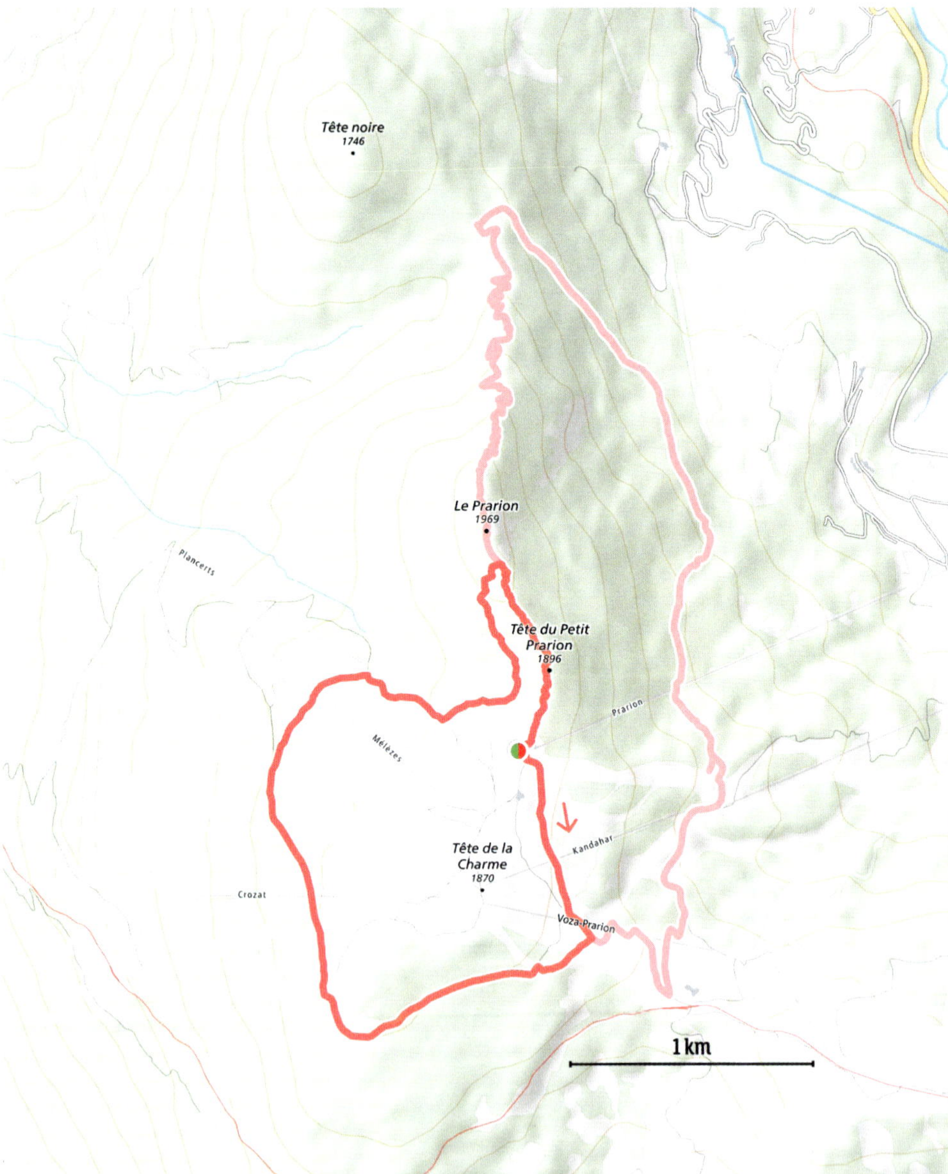
Tête noire
1746
Le Prarion
1969
Plancerts
Tête du Petit Prarion
1896
Prarion
Mélèzes
Kandahar
Tête de la Charme
1870
Crozat
Voza-Prarion
1 km

LET'S RUN!

Why we love it

The Prarion gondola takes you up to 1800 meters, making this the perfect run for a hot day. The route circles around Tête de la Charme on smooth, well-marked trails. At this altitude, you get clear views of the Mont Blanc massif and surrounding mountain ranges. The route finishes with a steep climb up to the top of Prarion, where you'll be rewarded by a 360-degree panorama.

Getting started

Turn away from the tram station and run to the crossroads, where you'll turn left, following a wide track downhill. At the next intersection, turn left again, following signs for La Charme. Pass under a chairlift and continue on this path for 800 meters. You'll have impressive views of Mont Blanc and Aiguille du Goûter ahead.

La Charme

Turn left at the fork, heading downhill and following signs for La Charme. After 100 meters, turn right at the fork, still following signs for La Charme. As you come out of the trees, you'll see Saint-Gervais below and Mont Joly on your left. Continue straight, following signs for Croix de la Charme. As the path bends to the right, you'll see the Chaîne des Aravis and the Chaîne des Fiz. Continue following signs for Croix de la Charme, which you'll soon see on your right. At l'Abbaye, turn right to follow the single-track trail uphill toward Hôtel Le Prarion. After 300 meters, turn left down a grassy slope to visit Restaurant La Cha. Alternatively, continue straight up the main path, passing under a chairlift. Turn right as you reach the larger gravel track, following signs for Hôtel Le Prarion.

Prarion

As you reach the crest of the hill, you'll see Mont Blanc ahead of you. Turn left here on the smaller grassy path, now following signs for Le Prarion. The path becomes rocky here, and you'll climb for around 130 vertical meters. The top is marked by a signpost and a viewpoint indicator that allows you to identify the mountains you're looking at. You'll have a spectacular view of the Mont Blanc massif and surrounding mountain ranges. This is a great vantage point from which to spot other runs, such as Mont Joly, Aiguillette des Houches, Pormenaz, and the Dérochoir.

Les Houches

Final stretch

Head back the same way until you reach the fork. Turn left here, following signs for the Télécabine du Prarion.

Bonus kms

Add an additional 6 kilometers and 450 meters of vertical gain by continuing along the Prarion ridge and down into the forest to Col de la Forclaz. From there, contour below Le Prarion to Chalet Du Délevret. At the chalet, take a right turn to head back toward the Prarion gondola. Finish by ascending the wide path you started on.

Pro tip

You won't regret stopping off at Restaurant La Cha. This family-run restaurant serves cold drinks and homemade cakes. If you can stomach something larger, they serve a range of colorful salads using cheese and cold meats from local farms, as well as heavier dishes such as burgers, steaks, and quenelles, which are a kind of dumpling made of creamed fish or meat, sometimes served with breadcrumbs and egg. The terrace has a spectacular view of the Aravis, and the ambience is tranquil.

15 LAC VERT

A run through quiet forest to the beautiful green lake above Servoz

STATISTICS

↔ Distance 11km ↑ Ascent 671 ↓ Descent 671m High point 1434m

DIFFICULTY

1

TECHNICALITY

COUNTRY

WHEN CAN I RUN IT?

JAN | FEB | MAR | **APR** | **MAY** | **JUN** | **JUL** | **AUG** | **SEP** | **OCT** | **NOV** | DEC

STYLE

90% Forest Trail 10% Road

POPULARITY

★ ★

ACCESS

Parking is available at the train station and opposite the Restaurant Gorges de la Diosaz.

REFUELING

Refuge Le Châtelet d'Ayères and the Restaurant du Lac Vert serve food and drinks. They are open from mid-June to mid-September. In Servoz, there's a store, a bakery, and restaurants.

BAIL-OUT OPTIONS

At either of two junctions before the left turn to Le Gouet, turn left to head back down to Servoz via Le Mont. You can shorten this route by 7 km by starting and finishing at the La Côte parking area. La Côte is accessible by bus. Just above the La Côte parking area, turn right up the steep trail, signed "Lac Vert par itinéraire escarpé." Turn left when you hit the jeep track to rejoin the main route and descend to Lac Vert.

RACES

Trail du Tour des Fiz

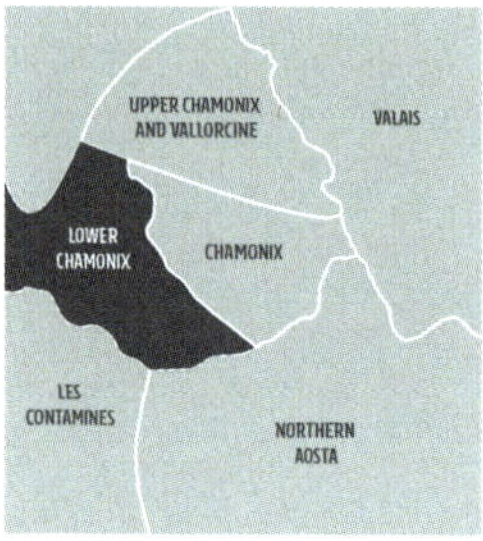
UPPER CHAMONIX AND VALLORCINE
VALAIS
LOWER CHAMONIX
CHAMONIX
LES CONTAMINES
NORTHERN AOSTA

PROFILE

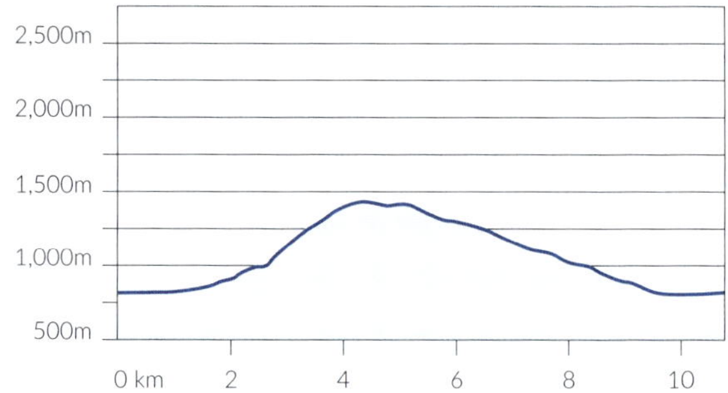
2,500m
2,000m
1,500m
1,000m
500m
0 km
2
4
6
8
10

Barmus
Les Mollays
Barmus
La Cote
Tête de la Fontaine
1206
Servoz
N 205
1 km

LET'S RUN!

Why we love it

The calm green waters of Lac Vert extend out from the base of the high cliffs of the Fiz, offering a stunning scene. Though the lake can be busy at times, the route up from the village of Servoz is quiet. You'll follow the Souay river steeply uphill before rising above the tree line and coming into view of the Mont Blanc massif.

Getting started

From the Servoz train station, run along the road to Le Bouchet, then fork right through the village center, heading straight at the crossroads and past Restaurant Gorges de la Diosaz. Turn right up a footpath to cut off a bend in the road. Rejoin the road, then turn right up to the hamlet of Les Moulins d'en Haut. Turn right onto a jeep track to cross the river Souay and join a single-track trail. Turn left, following signs for La Fontaine, then descend briefly to Pont de Chouay.

Lac Vert

From the bridge, turn right, following signs for Ayères, to start climbing steeply along the Souay River. Continue uphill toward Ayères at two more junctions. At 1440 meters elevation, turn left toward Le Gouet. After crossing the meadow at Le Gouet, turn left onto the jeep track toward Refuge Le Châtelet d'Ayères, where you'll have great views of Mont Blanc. A few meters after the refuge, head down the jeep track toward Lac Vert.

Gouille du Bë and Gouille Noire

When you're ready to leave Lac Vert, follow the jeep track down to the La Côte parking area. From there, take the footpath down toward Vieux Servoz. Turn left, following signs for Gouille du Bë and Gouille Noire, two more lakes. Stay on the main trail until the next junction, where you'll turn right to skirt around the right side of Gouille de Bë. Next, a gradual incline will bring you to Gouille Noire. Head around the left side of this second lake, staying on the main trail, which ascends a short steep hill. Follow the "A fleur de coteau" footpath signs downhill to Vieux Servoz.

Final stretch

Run down through old buildings, passing granite water troughs and then crossing the main road to join Route du

Le Châtelet
Alt.1418 m

Pont des Lanternes. Fork left onto a jeep track that descends to the river, then turn left again. When you reach the main road, turn right to head back to the train station.

Bonus kms

Instead of turning left to Le Gouet, continue uphill, then turn right onto the jeep track heading to Les Ayères. Follow the jeep track under the Fiz cliffs and loop around to Plaine Joux. From there, follow signs down to Lac Vert. This will add about 4 kilometers of distance and 300 meters of vertical gain.

Pro tips

Follow the narrow path around the lake for a full tour of Lac Vert! You'll see how the lake takes its green hue from the reflections of the surrounding trees.

Try out the cookies and patisseries in Les Douceurs de la Sauvageonne, the Servoz bakery in the village center.

16 PIERRE BLANCHE AND PLAN DE BENOÏ

A ridgeline run with a fast, undulating single-track descent through blueberry bushes

STATISTICS

Distance 15km | Ascent 1044m | Descent 1044m | High point 1972m

DIFFICULTY

2

TECHNICALITY

COUNTRY

WHEN CAN I RUN IT?

JAN | FEB | MAR | APR | MAY | **JUN** | **JUL** | **AUG** | **SEP** | **OCT** | NOV | DEC

STYLE

90% Forest Trail   10% Alpine

POPULARITY

ACCESS

Accessible by bus and train. Parking is available at the Les Houches train station.

REFUELING

Chalets de Chailloux is a family-run buvette that serves drinks, snacks, and bread with local cheeses. It is open from June to September.

BAIL-OUT OPTIONS

You can shorten this run by 5 kilometers and cut out 400 meters of vertical gain by parking at Le Bettey. You can also shorten this route by turning right 800 meters after Chalets de Chailloux and then running straight back to Le Bettey.

RACES

Trail des Aiguilles Rouges

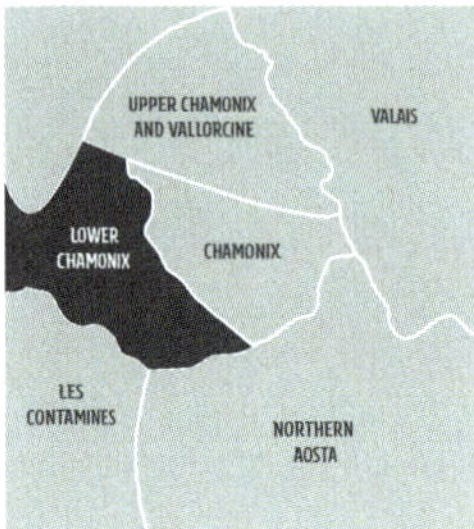
UPPER CHAMONIX AND VALLORCINE
VALAIS
LOWER CHAMONIX
CHAMONIX
LES CONTAMINES
NORTHERN AOSTA

PROFILE

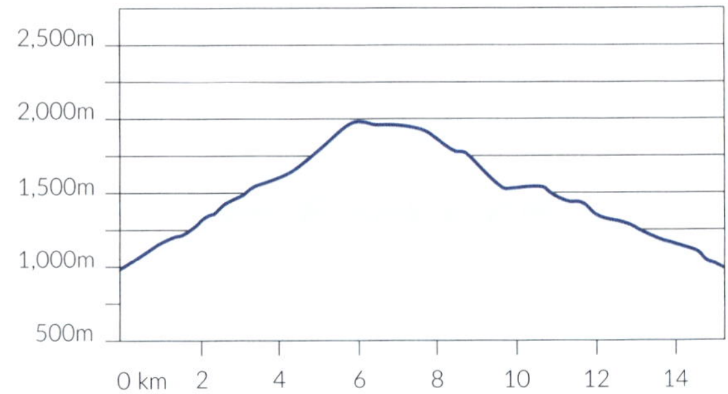
2,500m
2,000m
1,500m
1,000m
500m
0 km
2
4
6
8
10
12
14

Aiguillette des Houches
2285
Pointe de Lapaz
2313
N 205
Galerie d'...
L'Arve
Le Pont
Les Houches
1 km

LET'S RUN!

Why we love it

This run climbs up to Pierre Blanche before following the ridge just above the tree line and cutting down through Plan de Benoï, a beautiful alpine meadow. The trails are technical but not overly demanding, which makes this the perfect run to practice your technique on and to accustom yourself to alpine terrain.

Getting started

From the train station, follow the road that runs parallel to the train line. After crossing the bridge, take the footpath on your left, signed "Statue du Christ-Roi." Turn left at the next intersection and follow signs up through the forest to Le Bettey. When you reach the road at Le Bettey Parking, turn left to head uphill.

Pierre Blanche

Turn right at the next two forks, following signs to Plan de la Cry and Chalets de Chailloux. At Plan de la Cry, continue straight, following signs for Pierre Blanche. Continue along this trail for about 1.3 kilometers as it contours through the forest at a gradual incline. At Pierre Blanche, turn right to follow the ridge uphill. The trail is steep, and the trees give way to shrubby blueberry bushes and heather. Along this ridgeline, stop to take in the panoramic view—you'll see the Chaîne des Fiz, Pormenaz, Mont Buet, Aiguillette des Houches, the Prarion, Mont Joly, and as you rise higher, Mont Blanc!

Chalets de Chailloux

At the next junction, bear right to contour around the slope. This traverse is a highlight; fast and narrow, the track leads you through a steep and colorful moor called the "Plan de Benoï." At the chalets, turn right to continue downhill. Continue straight at the fork, heading in the direction of Merlet. At the next fork, turn right to continue downhill, now following signs for la Flatière.

Final stretch

You'll soon come to a right-hand turn, where you'll follow signs for Lac Noir. You can take this small detour to visit the lake or continue on to Le Bettey. Just after the parking lot in Le Bettey, take the signed path down to the right, into the forest. Turn left 500 meters later, soon passing a chalet on

the right. Turn sharply right at the next junction and follow the wide track to hit the Route de Coupeau just above the Les Houches train station.

Bonus kms

You can add 3 kilometers of distance and 300 meters of vertical gain by continuing along the ridge to the summit of Aiguillette des Houches from Pierre Blanche. We recommend that you come back down to Pierre Blanche—making this an out-and-back bonus—so that you can still enjoy the descent through Plan de Benoï.

Pro tip

Be sure to take in the short out-and-back to Lac Noir. The trail is quiet, and the tiny black lake is worth a visit.

The parking lot at Le Bettey fills up quickly on a nice day, so make sure to get there early if you are driving up to skip the lower section of the route.

17 PORMENAZ

Explore the wildest part of the Chamonix Valley with stunning views of the Chaîne des Fiz

STATISTICS

Distance 15km | Ascent 1268m | Descent 1268m | High point 2006m

DIFFICULTY

2

TECHNICALITY

COUNTRY

WHEN CAN I RUN IT?

JAN | FEB | MAR | APR | MAY | JUN | **JUL** | **AUG** | **SEP** | **OCT** | NOV | DEC

STYLE

60% Forest Trail 30% Alpine 10% Road

POPULARITY

ACCESS

Parking is available at the train station and opposite the Restaurant Gorges de la Diosaz.

REFUELING

The Refuge de Moëde Anterne is open from mid June to the end of September and serves a large range of local food and drinks. In Servoz, there is a store, a bakery, and restaurants.

BAIL-OUT OPTIONS

There aren't many options to shorten this route, other than turning back to Servoz. Refuge de Moëde Anterne is a fairly flat 2 kilometers north of Lac de Pormenaz if you need shelter and food.

RACES

Le Trail du Tour des Fiz

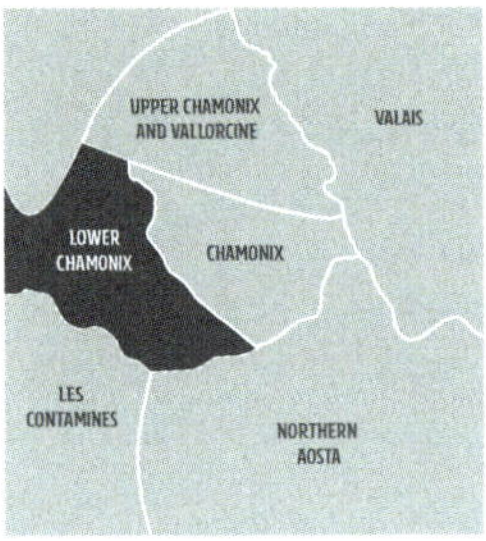
UPPER CHAMONIX AND VALLORCINE
VALAIS
LOWER CHAMONIX
CHAMONIX
LES CONTAMINES
NORTHERN AOSTA

PROFILE

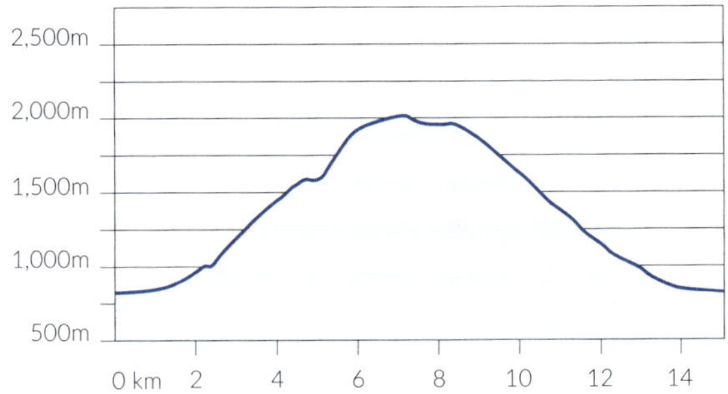
2,500m
2,000m
1,500m
1,000m
500m
0 km
2
4
6
8
10
12
14

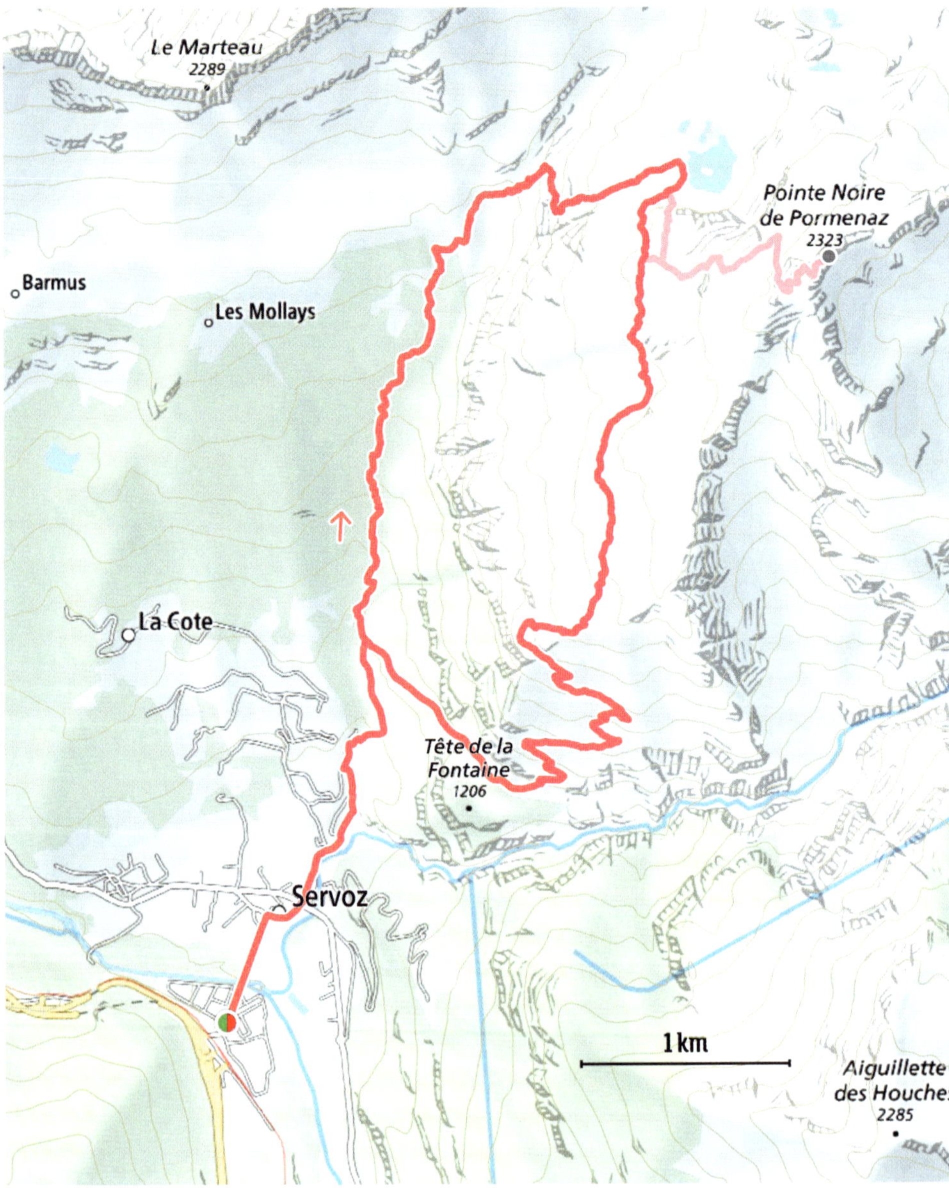
Le Marteau
2289
Pointe Noire de Pormenaz
2323
Barmus
Les Mollays
La Cote
Tête de la Fontaine
1206
Servoz
1 km
Aiguillette des Houches
2285

LET'S RUN!

Why we love it

Pormenaz is one of the wilder areas of the Chamonix valley. You'll see fewer people than on the lift-accessible mountains. Lac de Pormenaz is a beautiful Alpine lake set against the backdrop of the towering Chaîne des Fiz.

Getting started

From Servoz train station, run along the road to Le Bouchet, then fork right through the village center and continue straight on at the crossroads. Soon after, turn right off the road, heading up to Les Moulins d'en Haut. Turn right again onto the jeep track, then cross the river Souay. Ascend on a shady single-track trail before turning left onto a wider path, following signs for La Fontaine. Descend briefly on a jeep track to Pont de Chouay.

La Chorde

Beyond the bridge is a parking area where you'll find a public toilet in the summer. From the bridge, turn right toward Ayères and begin a steep ascent along the river. At the coming junctions, keep following signs for Ayères. Eventually, you'll turn right onto a jeep track, following signs for Pormenaz. At Chalets du Souay, turn right on a trail signed "Lac de Pormenaz" and "La Chorde." Cross a stream via a footbridge and climb uphill for 100 vertical meters. At the fork, turn right toward La Chorde. The path climbs up the gully, where there are metal ladders and handrails.

Lac Pormenaz

Follow the path on the right side of Lac Pormenaz toward Chalets de Pormenaz. At the next fork, turn right to traverse the side of the Pormenaz mountain. The trail is marked by yellow paint flashes on rocks. At the next junction, continue straight toward Chalets de Pormenaz. Follow the undulating path across the hillside, then descend gradually to the Pormenaz pastures and through a collection of farm buildings. There's a water fountain here, which you can turn on using the faucet underneath. Make sure to turn it off afterward!

Final stretch

From the chalets, continue downhill toward Servoz. Steep switchbacks bring you to a jeep track at La Fontaine, which you'll follow downhill before coming to another water

fountain on the left of the track. The jeep track continues down to a junction with a footpath that turns sharply to the left. Take this turn, following signs for Les Moulins, then retrace your steps back to the train station.

Bonus kms

You can add 3 kilometers and 280 meters of vertical gain by summiting the Pointe Noire de Pormenaz. This trail isn't signed, but you'll see the path forking to the left when you've run about 200 meters from Lac de Pormenaz. You'll start on a rocky path that's fenced in by a chain and soon come to a big rock slab, which you'll run across. You'll join the trail that heads up from the right at about 2090 meters. Continue following the yellow paint marks until you reach the top. From the summit, you'll descend on the same path, but you can fork left at 2090 meters to stay on the main trail and come to a junction where you can turn left to traverse to Chalets de Pormenaz.

Pro tip

There are usually large, fluffy "Patou" dogs guarding the flocks of sheep on the Pormenaz. If you see them, keep your distance, avoid getting between the dogs and the sheep, and slow to a walk.

18 TÊTE ROUSSE

Mix with mountaineers on this technical, high-elevation adventure to the top of Les Rognes and beyond

STATISTICS

↔ Distance 15km   Ascent 1438m   Descent 1438m   High point 3167m

DIFFICULTY

3

TECHNICALITY

COUNTRY

WHEN CAN I RUN IT?

JAN | FEB | MAR | APR | MAY | JUN | JUL | **AUG** | **SEP** | OCT | NOV | DEC

STYLE

70% Alpine   30% Forest Trail

POPULARITY

ACCESS

Accessible by bus and train (note that the train station is 1.2 kilometers from the lift station). Take the train to the Viaduc Sainte-Marie stop. Parking is available at Parking de Bellevue, Les Houches. This run is lift-assisted, so start by riding the Télécabine de Bellevue.

REFUELING

This run starts and finishes at the top of the Bellevue Cable Car, where there is a full-service buvette. Refuge de Tête Rousse is the high point of this course and you'll pass Refuge du Nid d'Aigle on your descent. Both serve drinks, tarts, and hot meals.

BAIL-OUT OPTIONS

After going over the top of Les Rognes (2800 meters), this run follows an out-and-back route to the Tête Rousse hut, so you can opt to descend quickly to Nid d'Aigle instead of continuing up to Tête Rousse. You can also take the cog railway from the Nid d'Aigle back to Bellevue.

RACES

La Montée du Nid d'Aigle

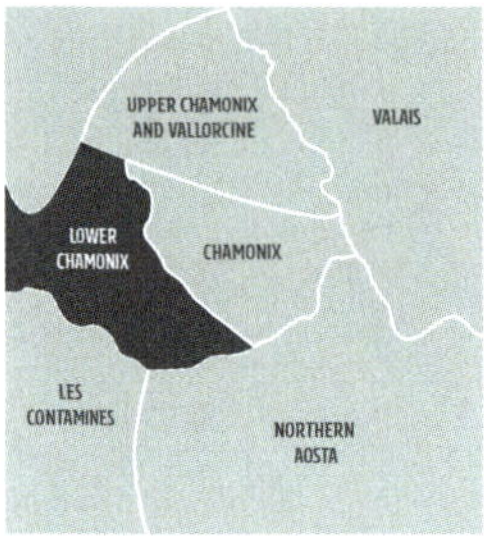
UPPER CHAMONIX AND VALLORCINE
VALAIS
LOWER CHAMONIX
CHAMONIX
LES CONTAMINES
NORTHERN AOSTA

PROFILE

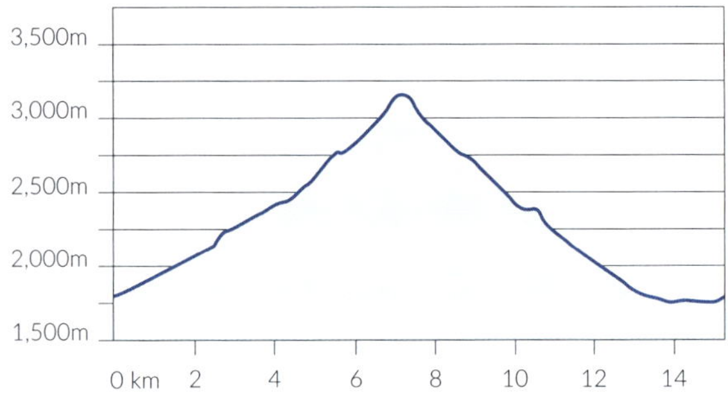
3,500m
3,000m
2,500m
2,000m
1,500m
0 km
2
4
6
8
10
12
14

Le Pont
Les Houches
Arve
Bellevue
Bellevue
1801
Mont Lachat
2115
Les Rognes
2853
Refuge de Tête Rousse
3167
1 km
Pointe Inférieure
2830

LET'S RUN!

Why we love it

This high-elevation alpine route features a high point of this guidebook. It's not only a varied, fun, and technical run but also provides a glimpse into the world of mountaineering: the regular route up Mont Blanc begins at the Nid d'Aigle and passes the Tête Rousse Hut. On this rocky, lunar, high-elevation terrain, you'll likely come across some of the many ibex that live up in these parts, away from the bustle of the lower elevations.

Getting started

From the top of the Bellevue cable car, head behind the building and take the left-hand trail, which offers a great warm-up traverse across the northern flank of Mont Lachat. On the far side of the mountain, you'll reach the Col du Mont Lachat and a cog railway stop. Follow the railway uphill, staying on its left until you reach a red trail sign for Les Rognes, which you'll follow onto an alpine trail.

Les Rognes

This well-defined trail runs parallel to the train tracks for a while before hooking back left across the slope for a long traverse. A series of steep switchbacks will bring you to a promontory with a large ornate cross. From here to the top, the terrain is rough and the trail is marked by painted yellow blazes on rocks. Moving through the rocks, the trail zigzags to avoid sections of tricky terrain and loose rocks and scree. If you have to traverse any *névés* (snowfields), we encourage you to turn back. This is a no-fall zone. As you continue, you'll come to several chains, and finally a small ladder bolted to the rocks. Soon after, you'll find yourself at the top of Les Rognes.

Onto the regular route up Mont Blanc

After cresting the ridge, follow blazes and cairns down to a big rocky plateau and a junction. Go straight across the plateau toward Tête Rousse on a vague trail. On the far side, the trail becomes more defined and is clearly marked by blazes as it heads up a rocky ridge. Though less technical than Les Rognes, it's steep, and you'll have to use your hands to move through the rocks. At the high point, you'll see an antenna and a large snowfield with a well-defined track leading to the Tête Rousse Hut. On the left is the "Brigade Blanche" cabin, where gendarmes verify gear and hut reservations before letting people continue. If they ask, tell them you are only going to Tête Rousse.

Leaving the alpine zone

Traverse to the hut for a snack and an impressive view of the face of Bionnassay to the south. Head back down the way you came until you reach a junction with signs for Nid d'Aigle. From here, you'll see many trails braiding through the rocky terrain. Follow the blazes and cairns downhill to a 4x4 road and the Nid d'Aigle train station. Head left to the refuge, then traverse the slope and descend steeply. You can continue to a lookout point near the Bionnassay glacier, but you'll have to return to the main path to descend.

Final stretch

The trail picks its way down the slope on some stairs and a small ladder. It traverses the moraine into the forest before reaching a big open grassy basin. Traverse on the trail until you join the Tour du Mont-Blanc, heading to Bellevue. The trail then reenters the forest and traverses, climbing gently. At each junction, continue to follow signs to Bellevue. You'll crest the ridge, cross the train tracks, and find yourself back at the start.

Bonus kms

If you want to add about 5 kilometers and 900 more meters of vert, you can begin this route from the valley floor! Starting from the Les Houches Tourism Office, you can follow the road uphill past the cemetery to the hamlet of Les Gens. From there, take the trail that follows the Griaz stream and then heads up an old moraine in the forest. Continue past Les Lanchers and the Baraque Forestière des Arandellys. Take the well-marked trail that climbs steeply and then traverses right before joining the main route before Col du Mont Lachat. You can follow the same route on the way down.

Pro tips

Whenever you find yourself on steep terrain and in places where you may need to use your hands to pass over rocky sections, always check how solid the rocks are before you put your weight on them. If you knock down a loose rock, yell "pierre!" to let people below you know a rock is coming.

19 LE DÉROCHOIR

A strenuous run that explores the seemingly impassable Chaîne des Fiz via a series of notches, boulder fields, chains, and ladders

STATISTICS

Distance 23km | Ascent 1762m | Descent 1762m | High point 2344m

DIFFICULTY

3

TECHNICALITY

COUNTRY

WHEN CAN I RUN IT?

JAN | FEB | MAR | APR | MAY | JUN | **JUL** | **AUG** | **SEP** | OCT | NOV | DEC

STYLE

80% Alpine | 10% Forest Trail | 10% Road

POPULARITY

ACCESS

Accessible by bus and train. Parking is available at the Servoz train station.

REFUELING

Refuge de Platé is open from June to September and serves drinks, light lunches, and fruit tarts. In Servoz, there's a store, a bakery, and restaurants.

BAIL-OUT OPTIONS

You can shorten this route by 7 kilometers and 300 meters of vertical gain by starting at the La Côte parking lot. La Côte is also accessible by bus.

RACES

Trail du Tour des Fiz

UPPER CHAMONIX AND VALLORCINE
VALAIS
LOWER CHAMONIX
CHAMONIX
LES CONTAMINES
NORTHERN AOSTA

PROFILE

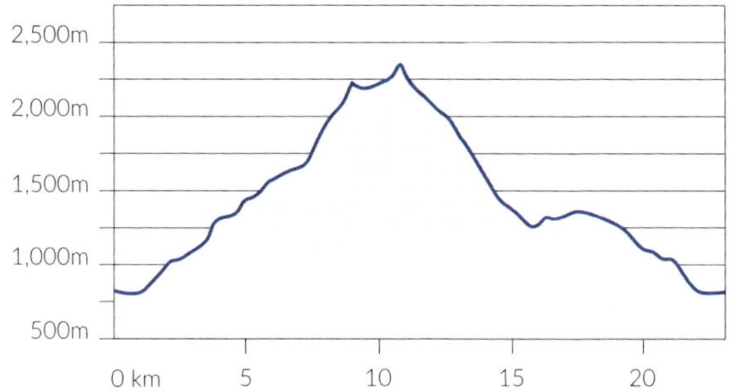
2,500m
2,000m
1,500m
1,000m
500m
0 km
5
10
15
20

Aup de Véran 2437
Les Grandes Platières 2480
Tête des Lindars 2560
Tête du Colonney 2692
le Sautet 2622
Refuge de Platé 2032
Pointe de Platé 2554
Pointe du Dérochoir 2411
Le Marteau 2289
Aiguille Rouge 2636
Aiguille de Varan 2544
Barmus
Barmus
Les Mollays
La Côte
Le Nant Cruy
Servoz
N 205
PASSY
Chedde
1 km
Marlioz
Mont Borrel 1303
Galerie d'Amenée EDF
L'Arve
A 40
N 205
Tête noire

LET'S RUN!

Why we love it

The Chaîne des Fiz is a band of striking gray cliffs opposite the Mont Blanc massif. Behind the cliffs is the Désert de Platé, a flat expanse of beautiful, rippling limestone. This run cuts through the cliffs on rugged, remote trails. It's an adventurous, full-on route through boulder fields and notches and down narrow, echoey gorges.

Getting started

From the train station, follow the road toward Servoz. Turn left after the bridge and drop onto a river trail. Follow this for 700 meters, then turn right uphill. Turn right again at the road and then continue straight at the junctions, heading uphill toward the trail. Ascend the steep trail through the forest, following signs for Lac Vert.

Mollays

Shortly after the La Côte parking lot, turn right to go up the steep trail signed "Lac Vert par itinéraire escarpé." After 1 kilometer, turn right on the wide jeep track and head toward Refuge Le Châtelet. From the refuge, turn left onto the small gravel track, following signs for Les Mollays. As you climb above the tree line, you'll see the Châine des Fiz ahead.

The "Passage du Dérochoir"

Turn right at the junction, following signs for Le Dérochoir. This track contours below the cliffs, and you'll have views of the Pormenaz on your right. Pass through a collection of stone buildings known as Les Ayères. A sign will indicate a steep left turn uphill toward the Dérochoir, which you will take. However, if you continue on the large trail just a little further, you'll get to a fountain which will be your last chance for free water until you get back down to Lac Vert. Follow the trail blazes over and around the boulders, heading to the right of a tall tower. Use the fixed equipment (metal steps, ladders, handrails, and ropes) to climb the final section. From the top, you'll see the Pormenaz, Aiguillette des Houches, and the Prarion. On the other side, you'll see the Désert de Platé.

Refuge de Platé

Turn left to contour around the scree slope. Keep left at the fork, following signs for Plaine Joux. After you've passed several large boulders, you'll see the final climb to the Col de la

Portette: a series of tight switchbacks ascending through a notch in the rocks. On the other side, descend carefully down the loose shale. You'll see the refuge ahead, and you might pass a flock of sheep and guard dogs. Continue straight down to the refuge.

Final stretch

From the refuge, head down towards Plaine Joux. The path cuts through the cliffs and becomes exposed. Cross the metal bridge and then descend the steep shale through a tight chimney. The gradient soon eases, and the trail becomes more runnable. Keep turning left at the forks, following signs for Plaine Joux and then Lac Vert. From the lake, follow the main trail down to Vieux Servoz and then head back to the train station.

Bonus kms

Add about 7 kilometers and 600 meters of vertical gain by continuing from Refuge de Platé to Col de Barmerousse, then down past Chalets de Varan and Charbonnière. This descent is slightly less steep and exposed.

Pro tips

On the final climb to the Passage de Dérochoir, take extra care to stay on route. It can be tempting to stray from the markings if you want to pass another group, but we don't advise it. The rock here is very slippery and loose; use the handrails, steps, and ropes that have been installed for your safety. There are often flocks of sheep with guard dogs on the descent to Refuge de Platé. These dogs may approach you and bark. Do not retaliate or become aggressive; instead, speak to them calmly and walk away slowly.

Do not go over the Dérochoir if bad weather is forecast.

If you can, do this run on a Sunday, when the Refuge de Platé serves barbecue sausages and reblochon fondue. All the ingredients are sourced locally and flown up by helicopter.

LES CONTAMINES

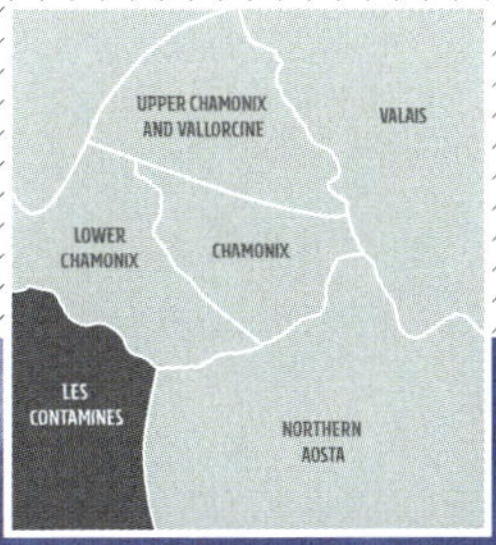
UPPER CHAMONIX
AND VALLORCINE
VALAIS
LOWER
CHAMONIX
CHAMONIX
LES
CONTAMINES
NORTHERN
AOSTA

20 REFUGE DE TRÉ LA TÊTE

Follow winding trails through a beautiful larch forest to reach a classic, high-altitude mountain refuge

STATISTICS

Distance 10km | Ascent 800m | Descent 800m | High point 1969m

DIFFICULTY

2

TECHNICALITY

COUNTRY

WHEN CAN I RUN IT?

JAN | FEB | MAR | APR | MAY | **JUN** | **JUL** | **AUG** | **SEP** | **OCT** | NOV | DEC

STYLE

90% Forest Trail 10% Alpine

POPULARITY

ACCESS

Accessible by bus. Parking is available at La Bottière.

REFUELING

Refuge de Tré la Tête serves warm meals, snacks, and drinks and is open from mid-March to mid-October.

BAIL-OUT OPTIONS

Retrace your steps or follow signs to Le Cugnon to return to your starting point.

RACES

None

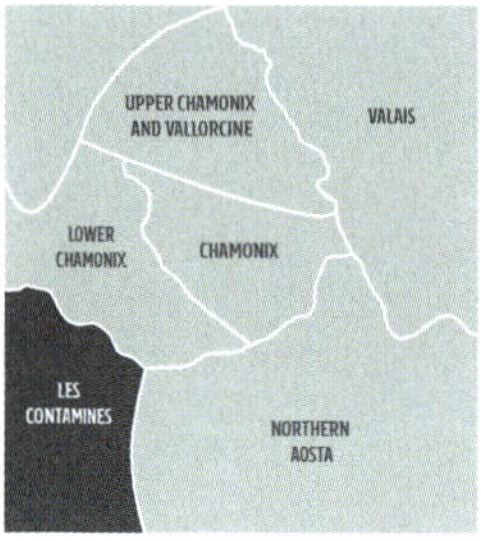
UPPER CHAMONIX AND VALLORCINE
VALAIS
LOWER CHAMONIX
CHAMONIX
LES CONTAMINES
NORTHERN AOSTA

PROFILE

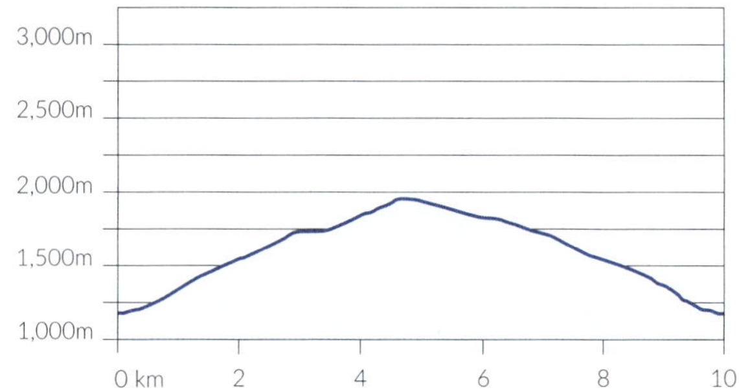
3,000m
2,500m
2,000m
1,500m
1,000m
0 km
2
4
6
8
10

Les Contamines-Montjoie
Le Lay
Pointe de Chaborgne
2754
Tête Noire
1973
1 km
La Laya

LET'S RUN!

Why we love it

Refuge de Tré la Tête is a popular stopping point for alpinists climbing the Dômes de Miage and other 3000-plus-meter peaks. The refuge offers a good selection of food and drinks and has private rooms if you want to spend the night! Expect panoramic views of Mont Joly, the Chaîne des Fiz, and the Tré la Tête valley.

Getting started

From the parking lot, head up the gravel road. Pass the public toilet, then take the path to the right signed "Tré la Tête." Keep following signs to Refuge de Tré la Tête at several junctions. Rising traverses will lead you above the tree line. Stay the course and follow signs to Refuge de Tré la Tête par la Forêt (you'll descend via the more runnable Chemin Bernard).

Refuge de Tré la Tête

Above the tree line, a final steep rocky section brings you to the stone Refuge de Tré la Tête, perched on the mountainside. Be sure to climb a few more meters up onto the hill just above the refuge for even better views! To descend, start via the path you came up on, then fork right onto the flatter Chemin Bernard. This trail is part of the Tour du Pays du Mont Blanc, a long-distance trek that covers a loop of 160 kilometers north of Mont Blanc, starting from the town of Sallanches.

Final stretch

At two junctions, follow signs down to Le Cugnon and then Le Cugnon par le Nant des Tours. The route takes long switchbacks on mostly smooth trails through the forest. Turn right to Cugnon, then cross the Nant des Tours stream. Continue downhill and left onto the gravel road to find yourself back at the parking lot and bus stop.

Bonus kms

You can extend this run by adding on an out-and-back run to view the glacier de Tré la Tête, or even continuing for 5km up to the Refuge des Conscrits. Both options are signed from the refuge. Note that these alternatives are not for the faint-hearted: the trails are technical and not always well marked.

Pro tip

This route is great to do when it's hot—it's in complete shade until mid-morning.

21 MONT JOLY

A striking ridgeline run above the Les Contamines valley, featuring woodland, meadows, and the 2525-meter summit of Mont Joly

STATISTICS

Distance 26km | Ascent 1730m | Descent 1730m | High point 2525m

DIFFICULTY

3

TECHNICALITY

COUNTRY

WHEN CAN I RUN IT?

JAN FEB MAR APR MAY **JUN JUL AUG SEP OCT** NOV DEC

STYLE

70% Alpine | 20% Forest Trail | 10% Road

POPULARITY

ACCESS

Accessible by bus. Parking is available at the Mairie parking area in the center of Les Contamines.

REFUELING

The Auberge de Colombaz serves drinks, snacks, and warm meals made with local produce and is open from June until the last weekend in September. There are various cafés and restaurants in Les Contamines.

BAIL-OUT OPTIONS

There are a couple of routes back down to Les Contamines from the ridgeline. The first descends just before Le Mottey, from the chalet after the Crêtet des Vernes. The second heads down after Mont Joly, from just before the Tête de la Combaz.

RACES

La Montagn'Hard
Diagonale du Mont-Joly

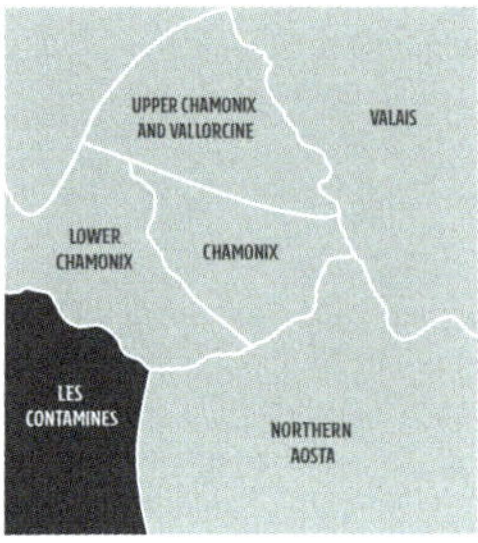
UPPER CHAMONIX
AND VALLORCINE
VALAIS
LOWER
CHAMONIX
CHAMONIX
LES
CONTAMINES
NORTHERN
AOSTA

PROFILE

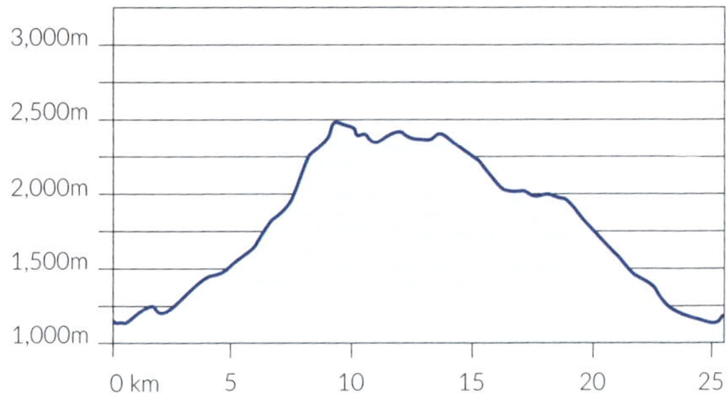
3,000m
2,500m
2,000m
1,500m
1,000m
0 km
5
10
15
20
25

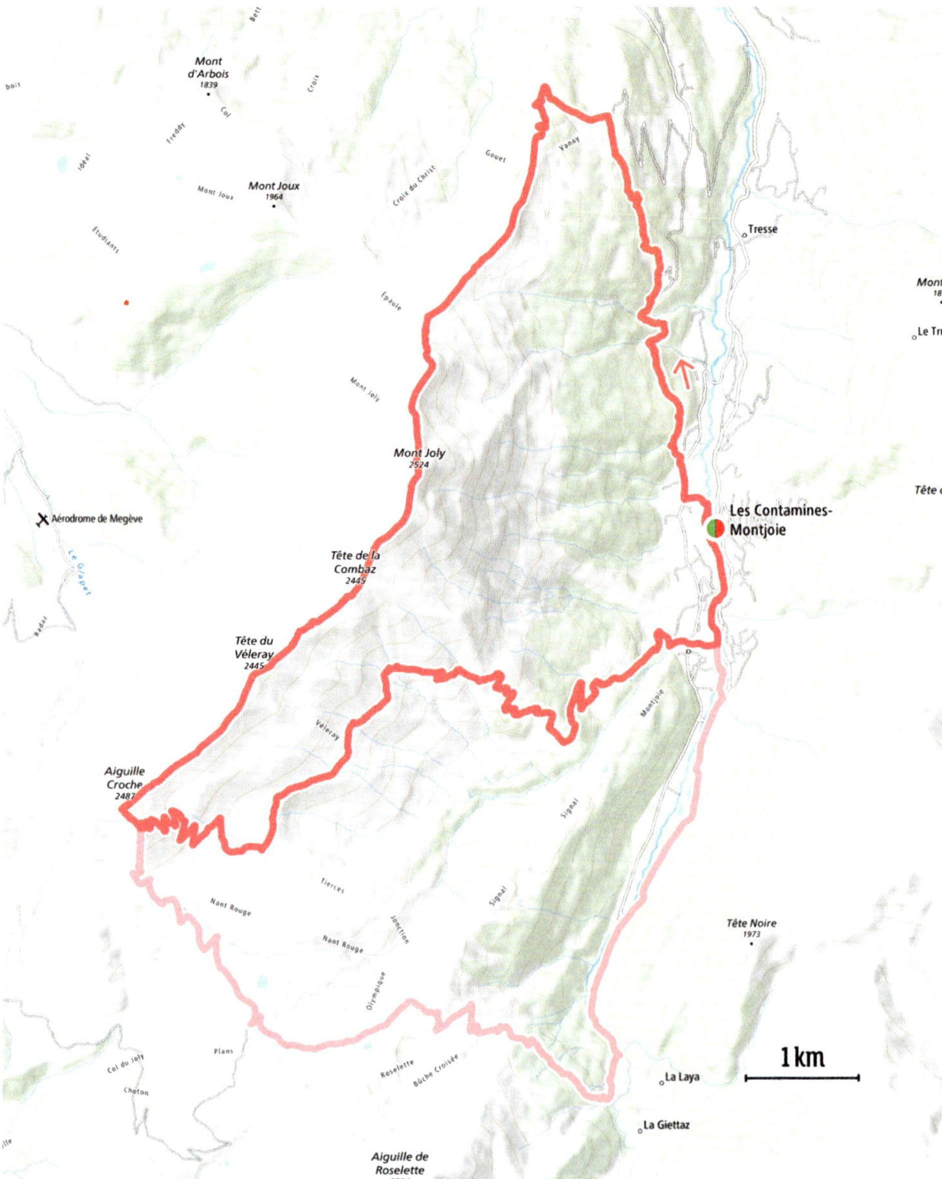
Mont
d'Arbois
1839
Mont Joux
1964
Tresse
Mont Joly
2524
Aérodrome de Megève
Les Contamines-
Montjoie
Tête de la
Combaz
2445
Tête du
Véleray
2445
Aiguille
Croche
2487
Tête Noire
1973
La Laya
1 km
La Giettaz
Aiguille de
Roselette

LET'S RUN!

Why we love it

This long ridgeline has panoramic views toward the Mont Blanc massif, the Chaîne des Fiz, and the Arve valley. The route is exposed, but there's always a clear path to follow.

Getting started

Head downhill, following signs for La Chovettaz. Shortly after you hit the river path, turn left over a bridge. Turn right onto the road, then turn off left, following signs for Saint Nicolas de Véroce and passing the oratory. Continue following signs to Saint Nicolas de Véroce as the path undulates and meanders across streams.

Reach old farm buildings at Le Carteyron and turn left at the intersection to skirt above them, following signs for Plateau/Plan de la Croix. At Entre-Deux-Nants, turn left up to Mont Joly and then to Plateau de la Croix at the Le Frêne junction.

Onto the ridge

At Plan de la Croix, follow signs to Mont Joly and head uphill on a jeep track. After 80 meters, branch right onto a path that leads up through a field. Rejoin the jeep track to reach the flatter Crêtet des Vernes via a steep climb. There's a water fountain at Le Mottey. Pass the top of the chairlift and ascend the steep rocky ridgeline, staying on the most defined path. As you run, you'll have a great view of the Vallée d'Arve, which leads to Geneva, with the Chaîne des Fiz to the right and the Aravis mountains to the left. After Mont Géroux, a flatter section leads you to the final steep push up Mont Joly. From the summit, continue along the ridgeline. You'll see the Beaufortain in the distance, with the Pierra Menta rock sticking up like a big tooth, and the Lac de la Girotte down below. Continue along the ridge, past La Combaz and Tête du Véleray.

End of the line

After your final summit, the Aiguille Croche, descend to the top of a ski lift, then turn left onto a jeep track. Take the jeep track down through the ski area toward Colombaz. As you near the farm at Les Tierces, turn left to traverse a runnable track flowing below the Mont Joly ridgeline. You'll cross several streams before descending. Continue downhill to La Tappée and a water fountain, then follow the jeep track down.

Final stretch

Turn left onto a gravel road and pass the Auberge du Colombaz. After 1 kilometer, turn right onto a forest path signed Les Contamines. Rejoin the jeep track, which soon turns into a paved road. At the river, take the gravel path left and along the river. Cross the bridge and then the road to continue on the gravel path. Take a sharp right uphill, following signs for Les Contamines center, to reach the car park where you started.

Bonus kms

After Aiguille Croche, turn right to reach the Col du Joly. Follow the jeep track to Signal, turning right to the Bûche Croisée before you reach it. Continue downhill to hit the Tour du Mont-Blanc just above Nant Borrant (there's a refuge here). Go over the Roman bridge and down to the chapel at Notre Dame de la Gorge. Coast back to Les Contamines on the riverside path.

Pro tips

Bring your poles—there's a lot of steep climbing to get to the summit of Mont Joly! Just make sure you have some way of stashing them in your running vest so you can enjoy all the runnable bits too!

The Auberge de Colombaz is famous for its Bougnettes, which are fried grated potatoes, similar to hash browns, and are well worth a stop-off. They are served with charcuterie and salad.

NORTHERN AOSTA

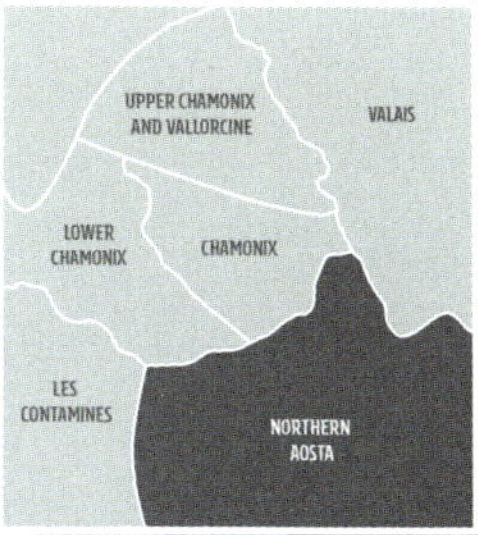
UPPER CHAMONIX AND VALLORCINE
VALAIS
LOWER CHAMONIX
CHAMONIX
LES CONTAMINES
NORTHERN AOSTA

22 MAISON VIEILLE

A gentle run with more descent than ascent and a chance to try some Italian food and coffee en route

STATISTICS

Distance 15km · Ascent 828m · Descent 1270m · High point 2418m

DIFFICULTY

2

TECHNICALITY

COUNTRY

WHEN CAN I RUN IT?

JAN | FEB | MAR | APR | MAY | **JUN** | **JUL** | **AUG** | **SEP** | OCT | NOV | DEC

STYLE

90% Forest Trail

10% Alpine

POPULARITY

ACCESS

From mid-June to the start of September there is a free bus service from Courmayeur to La Visaille. There is roadside parking in La Visaille, just before the barrier; however, note that driving in this valley is prohibited for non-residents during peak months.

REFUELING

Rifugio Maison Vieille serves drinks, hot food, and snacks and is open from June to September.

BAIL-OUT OPTIONS

The final steep descent can be avoided by taking the chairlift down and then transferring to the Dolonne tram at the Plan Chécrouit middle station.

RACES

UTMB Mont-Blanc
UTMB Mont-Blanc TDS
Gran Trail Courmayeur GTC55, GTC100

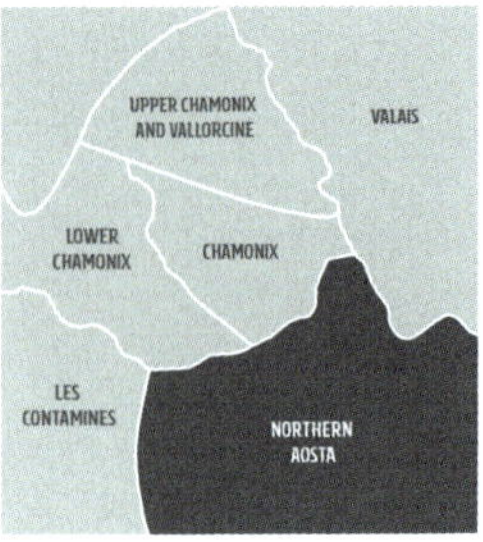
UPPER CHAMONIX AND VALLORCINE
VALAIS
LOWER CHAMONIX
CHAMONIX
LES CONTAMINES
NORTHERN AOSTA

PROFILE

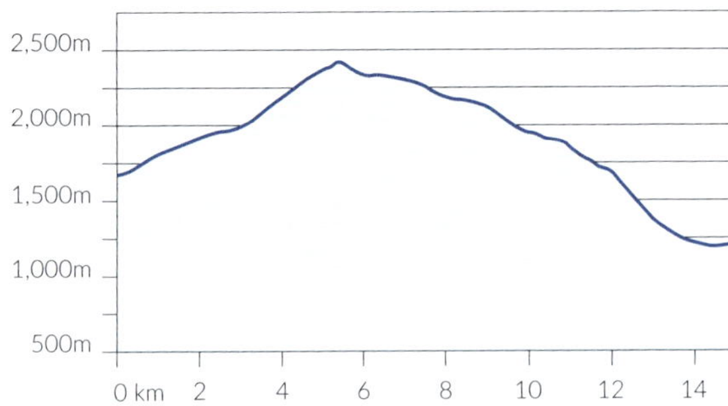
2,500m
2,000m
1,500m
1,000m
500m
0 km
2
4
6
8
10
12
14

Grand Pilier d'Angle 4243
Aiguille Blanche de Peuterey - Centrale 4112
Punta Innominata 3731
Aiguille Noire de Peuterey 3772
Aiguille Noire de Peuterey 2928
Mont Rouge de Peuterey 2941
Aiguille du Châtelet 2523
Skyway Monte Bianco
Meyen
Chapy
Val Veny
Mont Chétif 2343
Tête Neyron 2044
Dolonne
Start
Finish
Courm
Mont Brisé 2147
Tête d'Arp 2747
Tête du Grand Mont 2737
Tête de l'Ane 2789
Mont Fortin 2758
Pointe des Charmont Sud 2967
Mont Nix 2918
Mont de Nona 2075
Tête des Vieux 2856
Aiguille des Chavannes 2750
Tête des Jeunes 2784
Mont Berrio Blanc 3252
1 km
Mont Belleface - Punta Nord 2913

LET'S RUN!

Why we love it

This run starts with a short bus ride, which saves 400 meters of climbing. As a result, there's plenty of downhill—a combination of cruising through meadows and some fun, technical sections toward the end.

Getting started

From the La Visaille bus stop, head up the road and across the bridge. Take the signed shortcut through the forest, then continue on the road along the river. After 2.5 kilometers, you'll see the heaped moraine of the Glacier du Miage on your right.

Mountain pastures

Follow the road over the bridge, signed Rifugio Elisabetta. Continue for 100 meters before taking a sharp left uphill onto a single-track trail signed TMB and Maison Vieille. Cross a bridge and continue in the direction of Mont Favre, which you'll see up ahead. You'll pass through two pastures: Arp Vieille Désot and then Arp Vieille Damon.

Rifugio Maison Vieille

As you approach the top of the climb, the Mont Blanc massif appears in front of you. A beautiful, flowy traverse will lead you to the Courmayeur ski area. Pass Lac Chécrouit, then follow yellow TMB signs down a smooth single-track trail to Col Chécrouit. Maison Vieille will be ahead as you emerge from the trees.

Steep descent

Continue down across the meadow, following signs for Dolonne and Courmayeur. The trail skirts past the top of the chairlift before leading down to the hamlet of Pra Neyron. When you emerge from this cluster of buildings, follow the sign down and then head right across the meadows towards the lift station at Plan Checrouit. The trail runs around the side of the ski area and then to the left of the lift buildings and into the forest on a narrow steep path. This slope faces south, so it feels much more arid than the slopes you climbed up on earlier. You'll join the jeep track for a couple of meters before turning left to rejoin the trail in the forest.

Final stretch

When you hit the road, follow it down through Dolonne. Bear left at the first and second junctions, following yellow TMB signs. Just before the church, turn right to descend to the main road; then over the bridge for a brief ascent back to Courmayeur.

Bonus kms

Add 9 kilometers of distance and 440 vertical meters by starting from Courmayeur. This section mostly follows the road, with a few kilometers in the forest and on dirt tracks.

Pro tip

It's well worth stopping at Rifugio Maison Vieille for a coffee, homemade cake, or traditional hot dish. We especially recommend the cheesy polenta, which is made using a local cheese called Fontina.

23

COURMAYEUR DOUBLE VERTICAL KILOMETER

Give your legs and lungs a workout as you climb into what feels like another world

STATISTICS

Distance 8km Ascent 2190m Descent 0m High point 3466m

DIFFICULTY

3

TECHNICALITY

COUNTRY

WHEN CAN I RUN IT?

JAN | FEB | MAR | APR | MAY | JUN | JUL | AUG | SEP | OCT | NOV | DEC

STYLE

70% Alpine 30% Forest Trail

POPULARITY

ACCESS

Accessible by bus. Parking is available at the Skyway.

REFUELING

Pavillon and Punta Helbronner have modern restaurants with options ranging from café fare to gourmet meals. Rifugio Torino offers hearty Italian lunches.

BAIL-OUT OPTIONS

You can easily stop after a single Vertical Kilometer (VK) at the Pavillon mid-station and take the cable car or run back down.

RACES

Vertical Trail Courmayeur Mont-Blanc K1000, K2000 and T60 Trail Del Battaglione Gran Trail Courmayeur GTC 100

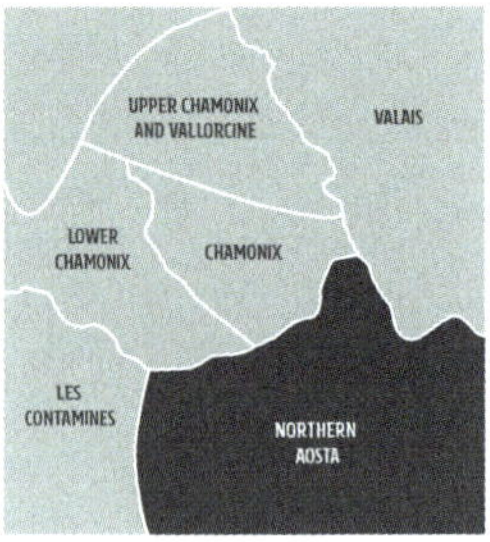
UPPER CHAMONIX AND VALLORCINE
VALAIS
LOWER CHAMONIX
CHAMONIX
LES CONTAMINES
NORTHERN AOSTA

PROFILE

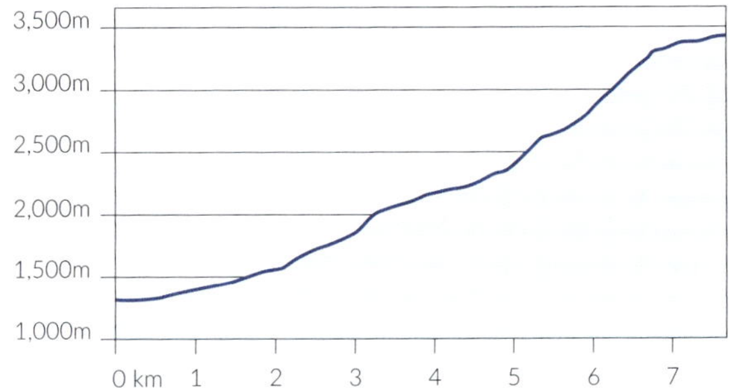
3,500m
3,000m
2,500m
2,000m
1,500m
1,000m
0 km
1
2
3
4
5
6
7

Grand Flambeau
3569
Pointe Helbronner
3462
Finish
Aiguille Rouge de Rochefort
3109
T1
Tour d'Entrèves
3118
Pavillon
3118
Skyway Monte Bianco
Chapy
A5
1 km
Start

LET'S RUN!

Why we love it

While the trail itself may not be the most beautiful one around, its novelty cannot be beaten. This route is a classic test piece that allows you to run straight from the valley floor to the high alps with no detours! It's also historically significant: In 1944, the Germans ascended this slope on their way to the Battle of the Vallée Blanche against French Resistance fighters. Keep in mind that it will be much colder at the top than at the bottom: Bring ample layers.

Getting started

From the base of the Skyway lift, take the pedestrian walkway under the road across a large parking lot. Take a right, following signs for the TMB onto a dirt road, keeping the river on your left. When the walkway curves left to cross the river, go straight onto the trail ahead of you, which may be marked from previous races.

Pavillon

Continue on the trail, crossing a small stream but always keeping the big river to your left. Cut back right to traverse across the slope before beginning a steep climb through the forest. When you leave the trees, you'll come to an interweaving of switchbacks and steep trails heading directly up the slope. Here, it's the runner's choice: Hundreds of vertical kilometer racers have worn direct trails, but both options lead to the same place. At last, a long traverse to the right takes you to the Pavillon mid-station, where you can bail, get food, use the bathroom, or visit art exhibits and the botanical garden.

Pylons and avalanche barriers

After Pavillon, the trail becomes less clear, and you'll once again have to choose between switchbacks or the VK test piece, which heads straight up a very steep grassy slope. The two trails rejoin one another before reaching a large pylon. From here, you'll leave the grassland behind and find yourself on a surface of rock and glacial till. Follow yellow blazes through the avalanche barriers, continuing under the cables. When you reach the first fixed rope, take a second to stow your poles.

Rifugio Torino

Stay on the prow below the lift and then eventually trend to the left. Pass through two more steep passages with fixed ropes. Gain the final ridge that traverses to the old lift station. From here, pass through the bowels of the building and back out the far side, taking the steep trail on the left to the Torino hut. And you've made it! The true Double VK route winds its way through the talus up to its high point, but we recommend taking the tunnel into the mountainside on the far side of the hut's terrace, which leads to an elevator that takes you up into the modern Punta Helbronner lift station with its impressive amenities.

Bonus kms

This route tops out on a glacier, so your run must stop at the top, where you'll take the lift down. Do not run back down the route.

Pro tips

Even if you see tourists walking on the glacier without specialized mountaineering gear, don't do it. Every year, people without equipment fall into crevasses just a stone's throw from the hut.

When the weather allows, it's a truly unique experience to take the Panoramic cable car across the glacier to the Aiguille du Midi.

There are lockers at the base of the Skyway, so if you arrive by bus, you can stow your things here before you head up the hill.

24 TIRECORNE

Run through spruce forest until you reach the tree line and then ascend through open fields to the old alp of Tirecorne

STATISTICS

Distance 8km | Ascent 725m | Descent 725m | High point 1945m

DIFFICULTY

1

TECHNICALITY

COUNTRY

WHEN CAN I RUN IT?

JAN | FEB | MAR | APR | **MAY** | **JUN** | **JUL** | **AUG** | **SEP** | **OCT** | NOV | DEC

STYLE

60% Forest Trail   30% Road   10% Alpine

POPULARITY

ACCESS

Accessible by bus from Courmayeur's Piazzale Monte Bianco main bus station. Parking is available at several Courmayeur municipal parking areas.

REFUELING

The Ristorante Baita Ermitage on the route serves traditional Aosta Valley cuisine, including local cured meats and cheeses, a full lunch and dinner menu, and a range of homemade desserts.

BAIL-OUT OPTIONS

This route consists of two connected loops, so you have the chance to shorten the run and still see the second half of the first loop.

RACES

UTMB Mont-Blanc ETC
UTMB Mont-Blanc YCC

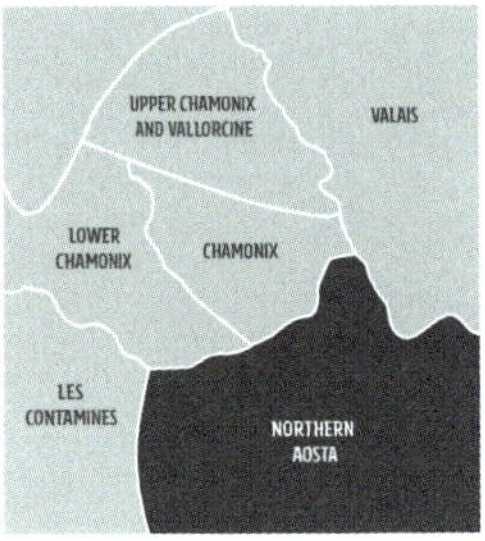
UPPER CHAMONIX AND VALLORCINE
VALAIS
LOWER CHAMONIX
CHAMONIX
LES CONTAMINES
NORTHERN AOSTA

PROFILE

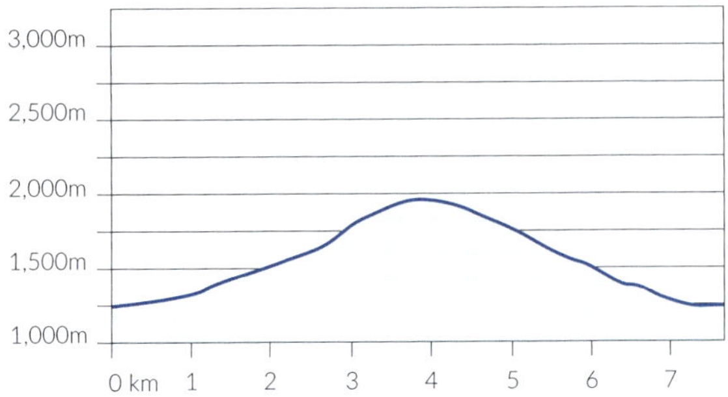
3,000m
2,500m
2,000m
1,500m
1,000m
0 km
1
2
3
4
5
6
7

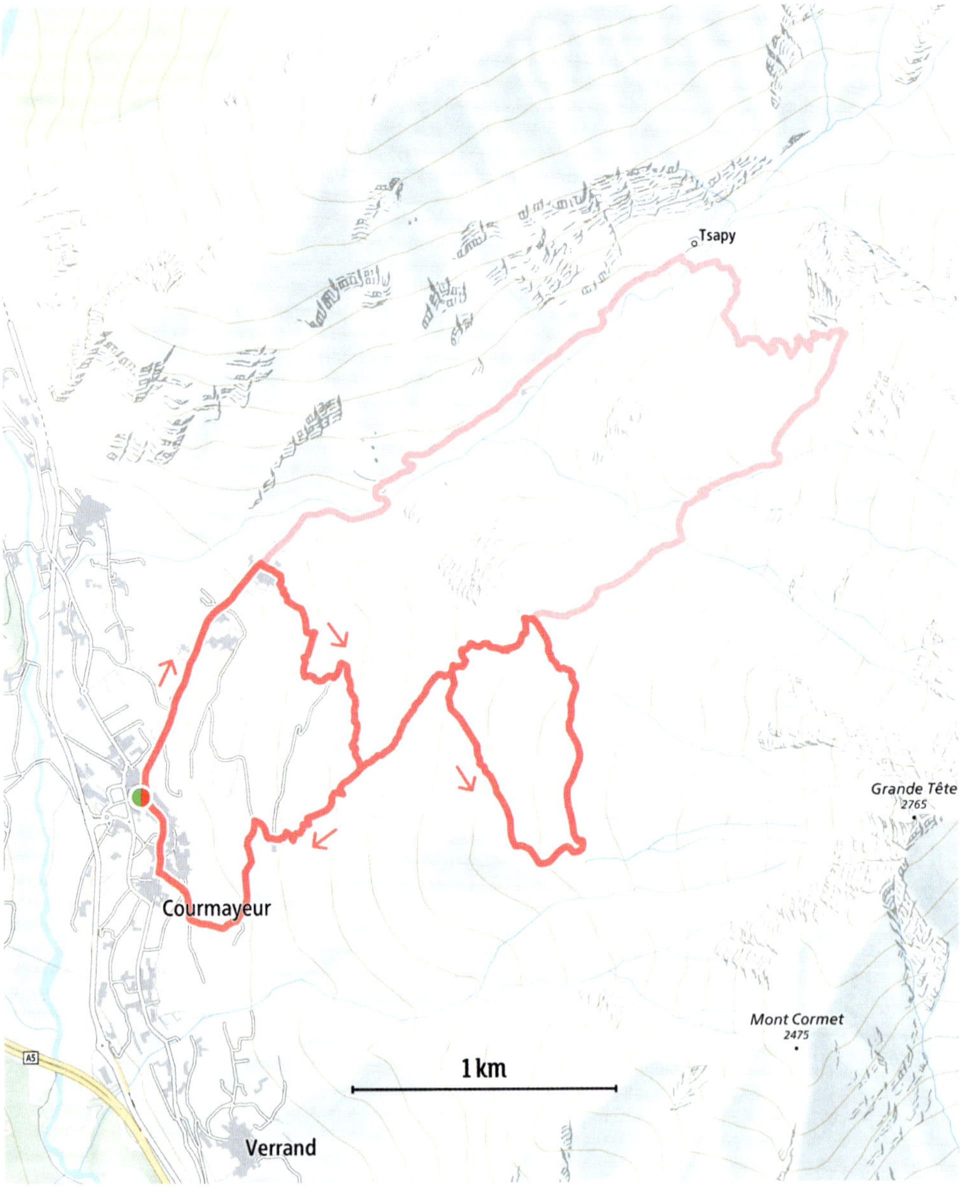
Tsapy
Grande Tête
2765
Courmayeur
Mont Cormet
2475
A5
1 km
Verrand

LET'S RUN!

Why we love it

A wise woman once said, "If you want to do a short run from downtown Courmayeur, it will mostly be a hike." Don't be fooled by the limited number of kilometers on this run: It's steep! That said, those who choose to tackle it will be rewarded by a dramatic view of the Mont Blanc massif, Mont Chétif, and Courmayeur.

Getting started

From the Alpine Museum on Via Roma in the center of Courmayeur, head uphill and out of town on the Tour du Mont-Blanc/Strada Del Villair for about a kilometer. Just after passing a water trough, take a right on Via dell'Ermitage, a narrow village road that soon turns into a nice single-track trail. Just before the small stone spring building, switchback left and right, following signs for the Ermitage. You'll soon come to a paved road. Pass Ristorante Baita Ermitage, a great eatery with a wonderful local menu and a beautiful view of Courmayeur and its surroundings. A hundred meters further on, you'll come to the large trailhead parking lot.

Tirecorne

A wide trail climbs through a spruce forest until it reaches a junction with the trail you'll take on your way back. Head left uphill; this section of trail is shared in both directions. At the next junction, take a right toward Tirecorne-Damon. Ascend steeply up to a large pasture, where you'll reach some ruins. From here, the views are breathtaking, but hold off taking photos until you finish the climb up the steep single-track path through the field up to Tirecorne, where there is a collection of stone houses, a bench, and a fountain.

Dortoire de la Suche

Weave through the buildings and then take the trail toward Suche-Damon. At this point, you'll finally get to run a bit, traversing the field and descending back into the trees, following signs for the Dortoire. The trees open back up to a fantastic view to the west. At the buildings, switchback left into the woods to rejoin the ascending trail.

Final stretch

When you reach the second junction, continue straight downhill toward Pussey. The trail hits a forest road; take a right downhill until you reach the paved road, which you'll follow for 100 meters before hooking back left on the road and then a trail until you reach the Strada del Pussey with its notably fancy homes. Continue downhill on the paved road, taking a right on Via Donzelli, which will take you back to Via Roma.

Bonus kms

From the Dortoir de la Suche, take a right to continue on the ETC race course, following signs toward Col Sapin (see page 170). From there, follow the trail and traverse the hillside, heading northeast until you reach a junction, where you'll take a left down to the hamlet of Tsapy. Then take a left down the valley to Tsappa and back to town on the TMB.

Pro tips

Because of the numerous fountains, you don't need to bring too much water on this outing.

Keep your eyes open as you hike up in the forest: Porcini mushrooms grow here in the fall!

At the end of your run, follow the pedestrian-only Via Roma to get a gelato at Crème et Chocolat!

25 COL SAPIN

Run up a moraine on switchbacks to the Col du Sapin, then descend with wide views of the whole northern Mont Blanc range

STATISTICS

Distance 26km | Ascent 1899m | Descent 1899m | High point 2523m

DIFFICULTY

3

TECHNICALITY

COUNTRY

WHEN CAN I RUN IT?

JAN | FEB | MAR | APR | MAY | **JUN** | **JUL** | **AUG** | **SEP** | OCT | NOV | DEC

STYLE

65% Alpine | 25% Forest Trail | 10% Road

POPULARITY

ACCESS

Accessible by bus from Courmayeur's Piazzale Monte Bianco main bus station. Parking is available at several Courmayeur municipal parking areas.

REFUELING

Rifugio Bonatti and Rifugio Bertone both serve snacks, drinks, and warm meals.

BAIL-OUT OPTIONS

After 5 kilometers, you can take a left down to Chapy (sometimes called Tsapy) and rejoin the road to town. Alternatively, after 8 kilometers, you can take a left from Col Sapin over Tête de la Tronche and Montagne de la Saxe and rejoin the descending trail at Rifugio Bertone.

RACES

Arrancabirra
UTMB Mont-Blanc
UTMB Mont-Blanc CCC
UTMB Mont-Blanc ETC
Gran Trail Courmayeur 100 km, Tor 450, 330, 130, 100, and 30.

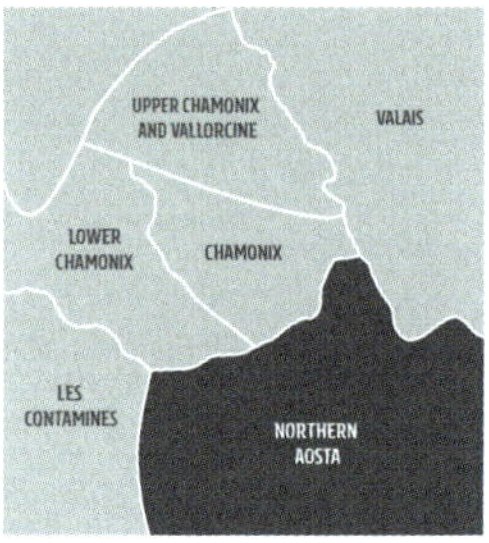
UPPER CHAMONIX AND VALLORCINE
VALAIS
LOWER CHAMONIX
CHAMONIX
LES CONTAMINES
NORTHERN AOSTA

PROFILE

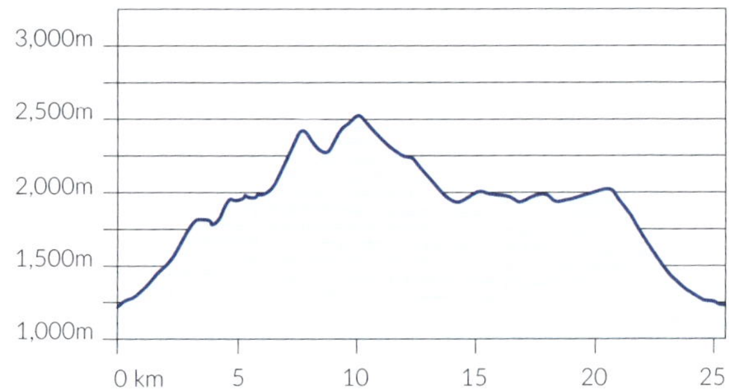
3,000m
2,500m
2,000m
1,500m
1,000m
0 km
5
10
15
20
25

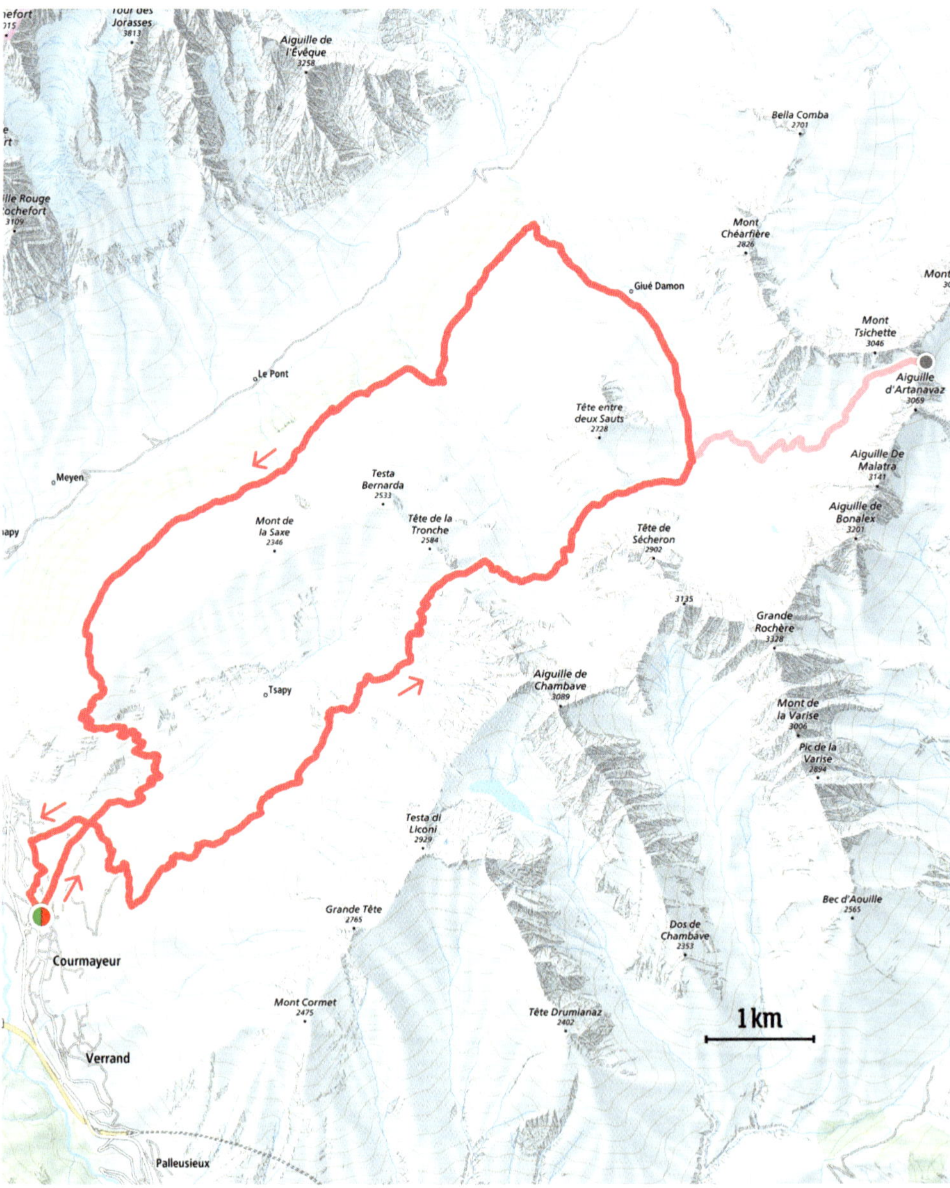
Aiguille de l'Evêque
3258
Bella Comba
2701
Mont Chéarfière
2826
Giué Damon
Mont Tsichette
3046
Aiguille d'Artanavaz
3069
Le Pont
Tête entre deux Sauts
2728
Aiguille De Malatra
3141
Meyen
Testa Bernarda
2533
Aiguille de Bonalex
3201
Mont de la Saxe
2346
Tête de la Tronche
2584
Tête de Sécheron
2902
3135
Grande Rochère
3328
Tsapy
Aiguille de Chambave
3089
Mont de la Varise
3006
Pic de la Varise
2894
Testa di Liconi
2929
Grande Tête
2765
Bec d'Aouille
2565
Dos de Chambave
2353
Courmayeur
Mont Cormet
2475
Tête Drumianaz
2402
1 km
Verrand
Palleusieux

LET'S RUN!

Why we love it

Parts of this route feature in nearly all the area's major trail races—and for good reason! The terrain is varied and provides absolutely stunning views of the northern Mont Blanc range.

Getting started

From downtown Courmayeur, follow TMB signs up the road toward Villair Damon. In the village, just after a fountain, take a discreet right onto via Ermitage. This narrow street quickly turns into a traversing trail, which you'll continue on, following signs for Ermitage. You'll soon briefly rejoin a paved road that takes you to the Ristorante Ermitage parking lot, where a right turn onto a wide trail leads you back into the woods.

Suche Damon

Take a left, following signs to Suche Damon, where you'll have your first big panoramic view. From behind the cluster of buildings, head toward Col Sapin, passing a fountain and entering the forest on a beautiful, traversing single-track trail. The path rises and falls, passing through several junctions; stay straight on the main trail toward Col Sapin.

Cols Sapin and Entre Deux Sauts

From here, the trees will become ever more sparse until you find yourself out in the open and in clear view of the steady, steep, switchbacking climb up a moraine to the ironically named Col Sapin (*sapin* means fir tree in French, but there are no trees to be found at the pass). Crest the pass and head down the braided trail on the opposite side, which leads across the head of the Arminaz valley. Cross the valley and then climb to the Col Entre Deux Sauts, your high point for the day, which affords fantastic views toward Col de Malatra and back toward Col Sapin

TMB: Bonatti to Bertone

From the pass, follow signs for Rifugio Bonatti through the alpine meadows of the Malatra Cirque, facing the Grandes Jorasses. Stop at the hut named after the world-famous Italian alpinist Walter Bonatti and enjoy the stunning view. From here, join the very popular TMB back to Courmayeur via Rifugio Bertone.

Final stretch

From the Rifugio Bertone, continue on the TMB down steep switchbacks into the forest and Val Sapin. Near the base of the valley, the trail crosses a dirt road a few times, cutting switchbacks until it reaches a sturdy bridge over the river. Take a right onto the paved road, which you'll follow downhill for half a kilometer until you reach the same village you came through at the start of your run. Just after the fountain, take a right onto Via Val Sapin, which joins a dirt road that you'll take down through open fields until you reach the tarmac. Take a left onto the road and then a right down through the beautiful Parco Bollini, which takes you back into downtown Courmayeur.

Bonus kms

After going over Entre Deux Sauts and descending into the Malatra Cirque, rather than heading left down to the valley, take a right and climb steadily up to the famous Col de Malatra, which is the final big pass in six of the Tor des Géants races.

Pro tip

Stop at the Rifugio Bonatti for a thick Italian hot chocolate with whipped cream. While you enjoy this rich treat, immerse yourself in the history of the region's alpinism and the stories of Walter Bonatti's famous climbs.

26 MONT FORTIN

Run up to the ruins at Mont Fortin for 360-degree views on a route that features alpine grasslands, wetlands, and an alluvial floodplain

STATISTICS

Distance 27km | Ascent 1929m | Descent 1477m | High point 2847m

DIFFICULTY

3

TECHNICALITY

COUNTRY

WHEN CAN I RUN IT?

JAN | FEB | MAR | APR | MAY | JUN | **JUL** | **AUG** | **SEP** | OCT | NOV | DEC

STYLE

60% Alpine 30% Road 10% Forest Trail

POPULARITY

ACCESS

Accessible by bus from Courmayeur's Piazzale Monte Bianco main bus station. Parking is available at several Courmayeur municipal parking areas. Regular buses operate from Val Veny back to Courmayeur.

REFUELING

Rifugio Elisabetta serves drinks and snacks and traditional lunches at midday.

BAIL-OUT OPTIONS

From Mont Fortin at 14.5 kilometers, take the steep trail that heads directly down to Val Veny and rejoin the descent at Combal/Lac du Miage for the final 4 kilometers.

RACES

Gran Trail Courmayeur 100km and 55km
La Thuile Trail Ultra 70 and Marathon 42
Tor des Géants 450 and 330
UTMB Mont-Blanc TDS

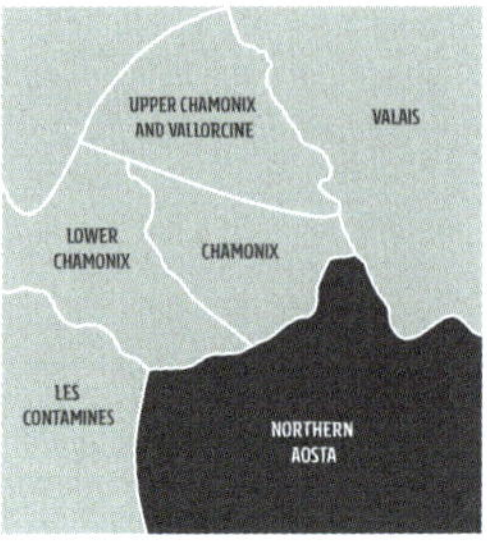
UPPER CHAMONIX AND VALLORCINE
VALAIS
LOWER CHAMONIX
CHAMONIX
LES CONTAMINES
NORTHERN AOSTA

PROFILE

3,000m
2,500m
2,000m
1,500m
1,000m
0 km
5
10
15
20
25

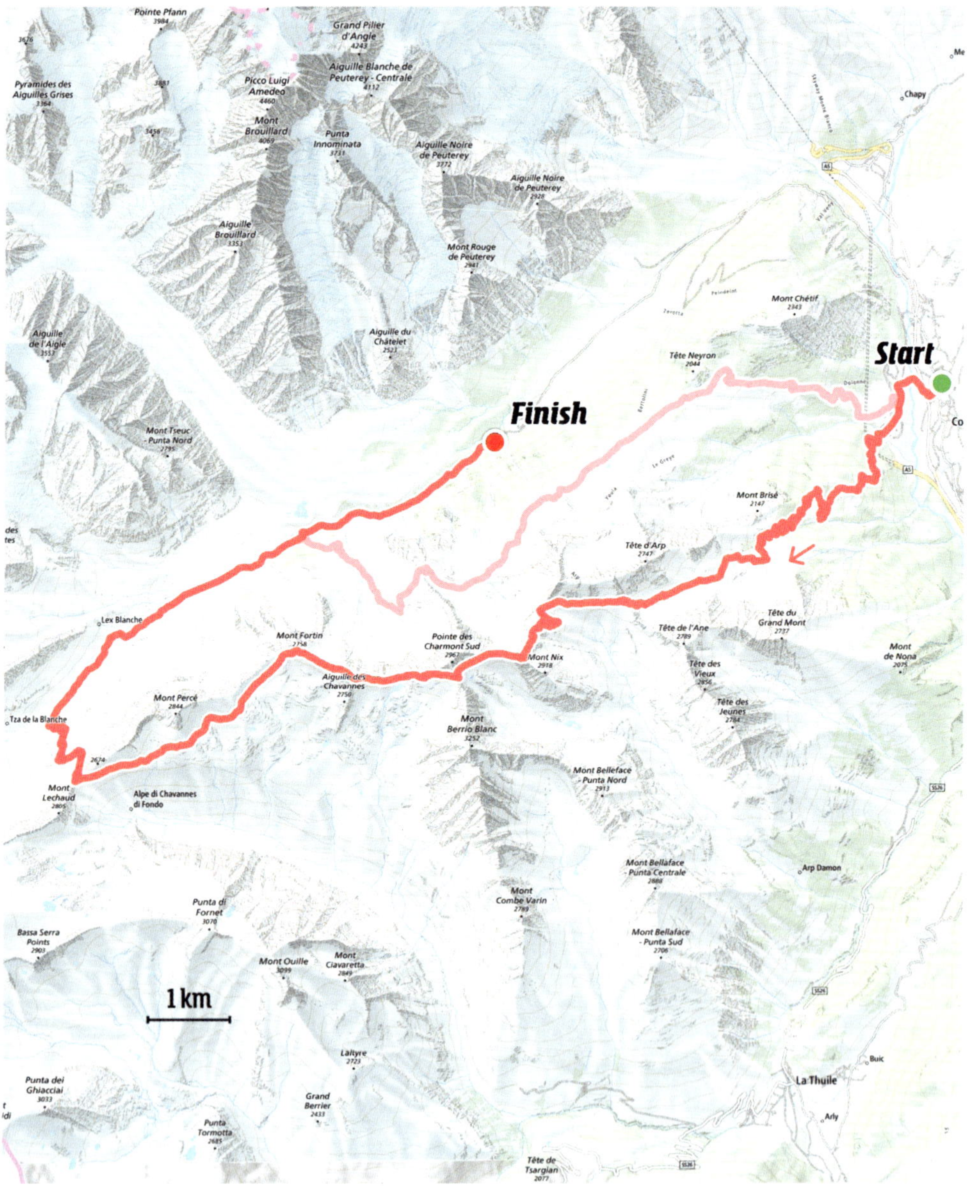
Start
Finish
1 km
Pointe Pfann 3984
Grand Pilier d'Angle 4243
Aiguille Blanche de Peuterey - Centrale 4112
Picco Luigi Amedeo 4460
Mont Brouillard 4069
Punta Innominata 3731
Aiguille Noire de Peuterey 3772
Aiguille Noire de Peuterey 2928
Pyramides des Aiguilles Grises 3364
Aiguille Brouillard 3353
Mont Rouge de Peuterey 2941
Aiguille de l'Aigle 3553
Aiguille du Châtelet 2527
Mont Chétif 2343
Tête Neyron 2044
Chapy
Mont Tseuc - Punta Nord 2795
Mont Brisé 2147
Tête d'Arp 2747
Lex Blanche
Mont Fortin 2758
Pointe des Charmont Sud 2967
Mont Nix 2918
Tête de l'Ane 2789
Tête du Grand Mont 2737
Mont de Nona 2075
Tête des Vieux 2856
Tête des Jeunes 2784
Aiguille des Chavannes 2750
Mont Percé 2844
Tza de la Blanche
Mont Berrio Blanc 3252
Mont Lechaud 2805
Alpe di Chavannes di Fondo
Mont Belleface - Punta Nord 2913
Mont Bellaface - Punta Centrale 2886
Arp Damon
Mont Combe Varin 2789
Mont Bellaface - Punta Sud 2706
Punta di Fornet 3070
Bassa Serra Points 2903
Mont Ouille 3099
Mont Ciavaretta 2849
Laityre 2723
La Thuile
Punta dei Ghiacciai 3033
Grand Berrier 2433
Punta Tormotta 2685
Tête de Tsargian 2077
Arly
Buic

LET'S RUN!

Why we love it

This wild and breathtakingly beautiful run begins on the historic Tor des Géants 330 race route and then continues along the ridge above Val Veny. Until the final descent on the TMB, this route sees much less traffic than some of the other runs featured in this book, and there's only one explanation for this: You have to work hard to get the places it takes you. But we promise the effort is well worth it!

Getting started

From downtown Courmayeur, follow the TMB route through the large roundabout and under the main road toward Dolonne. Follow Strada Della Vittoria to the left until it ends by crossing a bridge and opening into a small dirt parking area with benches and a fountain. Fill up your water here and then take the trail to the right with a sign for Col d'Arp.

Col d'Arp

A single-track trail climbs through the forest, sometimes steeply, passing through clearings and past ruins. After about 3 kilometers, you'll join a forest road that climbs up switchbacks through pastures with increasingly impressive views for another 3 kilometers. When the road flattens out and begins to traverse toward stone farm buildings, pick up the trail again on your left, following yellow blazes and markings for Col d'Arp, Tor, and 1A. From here, you'll climb through the valley—gradually at first, and then more steeply until you reach the pass.

Mont Fortin

Traverse to the right to the Col de Youla, where you'll have your first view of Val Veny and the south face of Mont Blanc. Soon after, Mont Blanc will slip out of view as you traverse the south side of the peaks and then climb steeply back up to the ridge. You'll play peek-a-boo with the Mont Blanc massif as you follow a traversing path. Before reaching Colle Berrio Blanc, you'll cut across the impressive but benign slopes of Mont Favre. While the path is clearly marked, be aware that snowfields can persist early in the season, which may mean you'll need to bring some form of traction. Continue along the ridge until you reach ruins on Mont Fortin and gain a 360-degree view of the surrounding mountains.

2
"Col des Chavannes"

Col des Chavannes and Val Veny

After Mont Fortin, a single-track trail drops down to the left, crossing alpine grasslands and a few wetlands where cattle graze. Shortly before the Col des Chavannes, you'll rejoin a traversing dirt track. Follow this until you crest the pass and then follow Alta Via 2 down switchbacks to the alluvial floodplain and the TMB. Follow the trail, passing signs for the Rifugio Elisabetta and some WW2 fortifications. After one last steep pitch with switchbacks, join the dirt road at the base of the valley. Follow this all the way back to Chalet del Miage, where you can take the bus back to Courmayeur.

Bonus kms

From Combal and the Lac du Miage, take a right onto the TMB, which you can follow over Col Checrouit and all the way back down to Dolonne and Courmayeur.

Pro tip

Bring enough water with you for a long day out! Because this route is at a high altitude and largely follows the ridgeline, once you leave the valley you won't see running water again until after the Col des Chavannes around 19 kilometers in (and even then, you'll want a filter).

Both French and Italian are spoken in the Aosta Valley, and trail signs can be a little confusing since spelling and language can vary. Sometimes the same pass will be signed as a "col" (French) and a "colle" (Italian). "Youla" is sometimes written as "Youlaz." Trust your instincts—these are the same places!

VALAIS

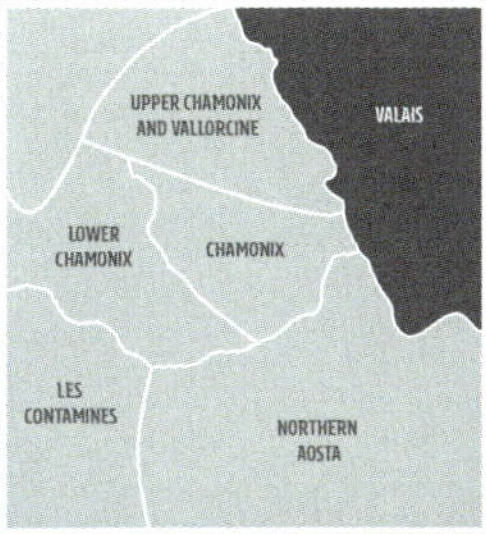
UPPER CHAMONIX
AND VALLORCINE
VALAIS
LOWER
CHAMONIX
CHAMONIX
LES
CONTAMINES
NORTHERN
AOSTA

27 MONT DE L'ARPILLE

A gentle, lesser-known forest run around the small peak of Mont de l'Arpille

STATISTICS

Distance 6km | Ascent 574m | Descent 574m | High point 2085m

DIFFICULTY

1

TECHNICALITY

COUNTRY

WHEN CAN I RUN IT?

JAN | FEB | MAR | APR | MAY | JUN | **JUL** | **AUG** | **SEP** | **OCT** | NOV | DEC

STYLE

90% Forest trail   10% Alpine

POPULARITY

ACCESS

Accessible by bus. Parking is available just past Hôtel du Col de la Forclaz, to the right of the road if you're coming from Chamonix.

REFUELING

There is no refueling available on this route. At Col de la Forclaz, you can get a cold drink at the hotel or an artisan ice cream from the farm shop opposite.

BAIL-OUT OPTIONS

Because this is a short loop, there isn't a bail-out option. Depending on where you are on the loop, either turn back or continue around.

RACES

None

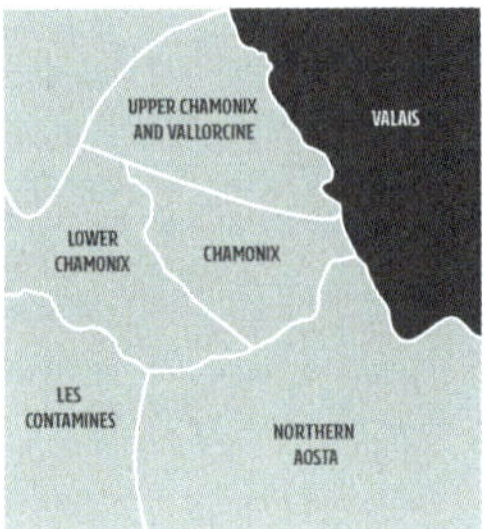
UPPER CHAMONIX AND VALLORCINE
VALAIS
LOWER CHAMONIX
CHAMONIX
LES CONTAMINES
NORTHERN AOSTA

PROFILE

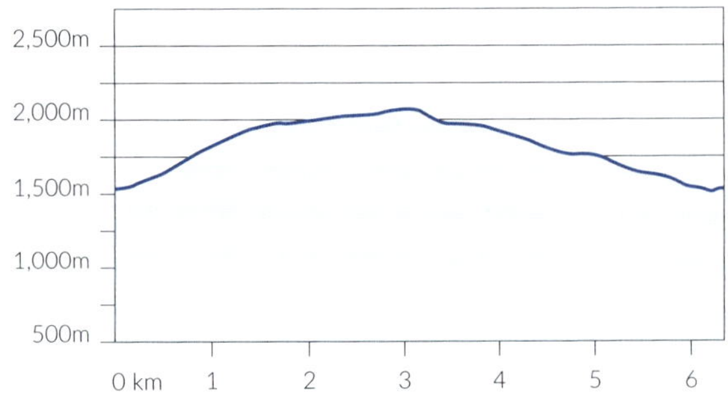
2,500m
2,000m
1,500m
1,000m
500m
0 km
1
2
3
4
5
6

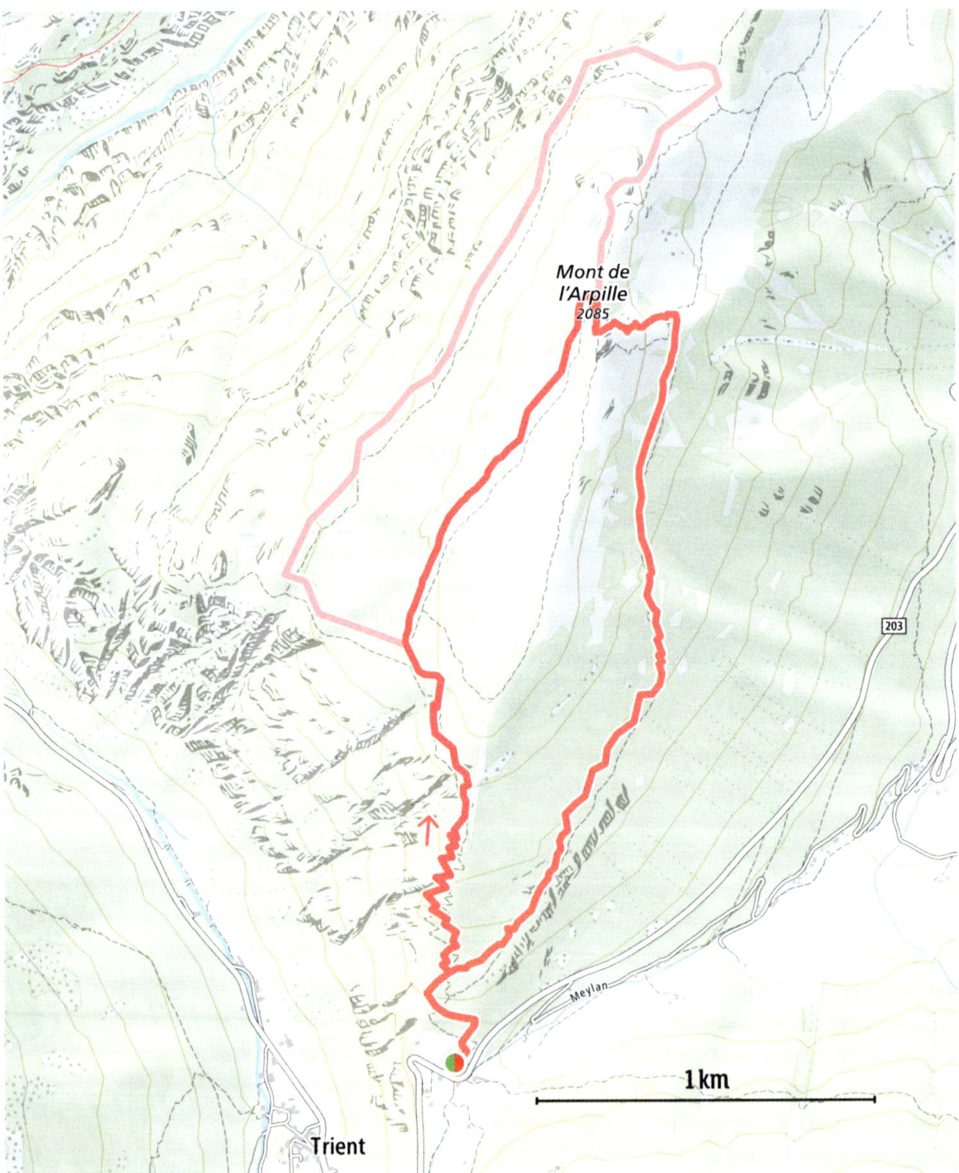
Mont de l'Arpille
2085
203
Meylan
1 km
Trient

LET'S RUN!

Why we love it

This run circles around Mont de l'Arpille, giving you a panoramic view of the surrounding peaks. Despite being so close to the road, it is a very peaceful route, and you're unlikely to see other people. The far side of Mont de l'Arpille feels wild and remote. The first trails are steep and rough, but they eventually ease off and become grassy on the southern slopes.

Getting started

From the parking lot, cross the road and follow the trail that departs from behind the Hôtel du Col de la Forclaz. You'll pass a big information board and continue along a metal fence. This first uphill section is steep, and the trail is covered in twisting tree roots.

Grassy contour

Turn left at the fork, following signs for l'Arpille. The trail soon narrows and becomes rocky. To your left, you'll see the Col de Balme on the opposite side of the valley. You'll pass a small scree slope and some exposed sections, but the trail is well marked. Continue straight at the junction, following signs for Mont de l'Arpille. The gradient soon eases, and the trees give way to shrubs and meadows. As you contour around Mont de l'Arpille, you'll see the town of Finhaut on the steep slope on the opposite side of the valley. One final climb brings you to the top. Stop here to enjoy the peaceful panoramic view. There's a map to help you identify the surrounding peaks, and there are benches to rest on.

Rocky descent

Follow the trail that leads in the opposite direction from the way you came. Turn left at the fork, following signs for Col de la Forclaz. Descend steep, rocky switchbacks for 300 vertical meters, then turn right at the fork to contour on a gradual decline to the Col de la Forclaz.

Final stretch

As you drop down into the trees, the path becomes steeper and rockier. Bovine will come into view through the trees, and soon after, you'll begin to catch glimpses of the Col de la Forclaz below. Rejoin the trail you started on and continue down to the road.

Col de la Forclaz 1h05min
Sex de Meylan
L'Arpille Alpage 25min
Chez les Proz 1h45min
Le Feylet Ravoire 1h50min
Martigny 3h05min
Le Revé 1h20min
La Crêta 1h45min
Grands Communaux 1h05min
Les Chesaux Ravoire 1h55min

Bonus kms

Add 2 kilometers and 200 meters by doing a more complete loop of Mont de l'Arpille. At around 1.9 kilometers, turn left at the fork to head downhill. Turn right at the next fork to contour around, passing through a boggy area on wooden bridges. At 4.6 kilometers, turn right and then right again, heading uphill. This will take you to the summit, where you can rejoin the main route.

Pro tips

If you prefer cruisy descents, do this route in the opposite direction.

At the top of Mont de l'Arpille, there is an information board that names the surrounding mountains. You can use this to identify a number of the other runs in this book.

The ice cream that is sold at the farm shop on the Col de la Forclaz is made using local ingredients from the Valais, such as apricots and blueberries.

28 LES GRANDS AND COL DE BALME

A mountainous but not-too-technical run that loops around the Trient valley, crossing from one side to the other below the glacier

STATISTICS

Distance 16km Ascent 1074m Descent 1074m High point 2201m

DIFFICULTY

2

TECHNICALITY

COUNTRY

WHEN CAN I RUN IT?

JAN FEB MAR APR MAY **JUN JUL AUG SEP** OCT NOV DEC

STYLE

60% Alpine 40% Forest Trail

POPULARITY

ACCESS

Accessible by bus. Parking is available next to Église Rose—the pink church—in Trient.

REFUELING

The Buvette du Glacier du Trient serves warm meals, homemade tarts, and drinks, while Chalet des Grands, a small refuge, serves only drinks and snacks. Both buvettes accept cash only. Refuge Le Peuty serves warm meals and drinks. Refuge du Col de Balme serves drinks, snacks, and warm meals, and is a good location to take a break, though it can be busy with Tour du Mont-Blanc hikers.

BAIL-OUT OPTIONS

To shorten your run, you can turn right at 7.8 kilometers to head downhill to Trient.

RACES

The Swiss Peaks 360
UTMB Mont-Blanc OCC and MCC

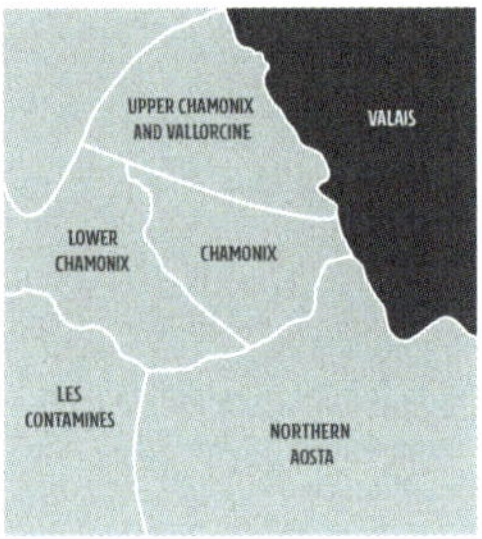
UPPER CHAMONIX AND VALLORCINE
VALAIS
LOWER CHAMONIX
CHAMONIX
LES CONTAMINES
NORTHERN AOSTA

PROFILE

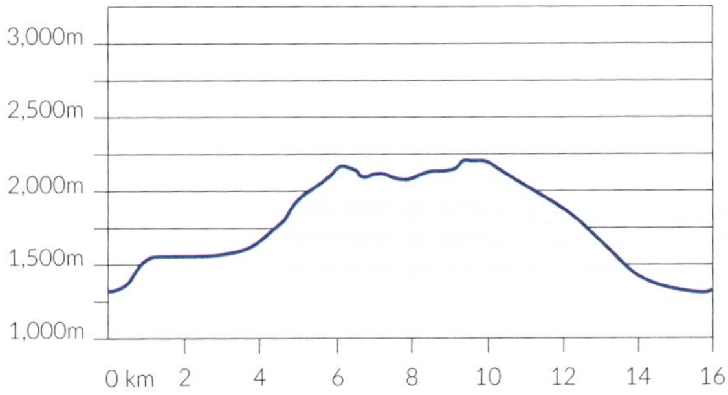
3,000m
2,500m
2,000m
1,500m
1,000m
0 km
2
4
6
8
10
12
14
16

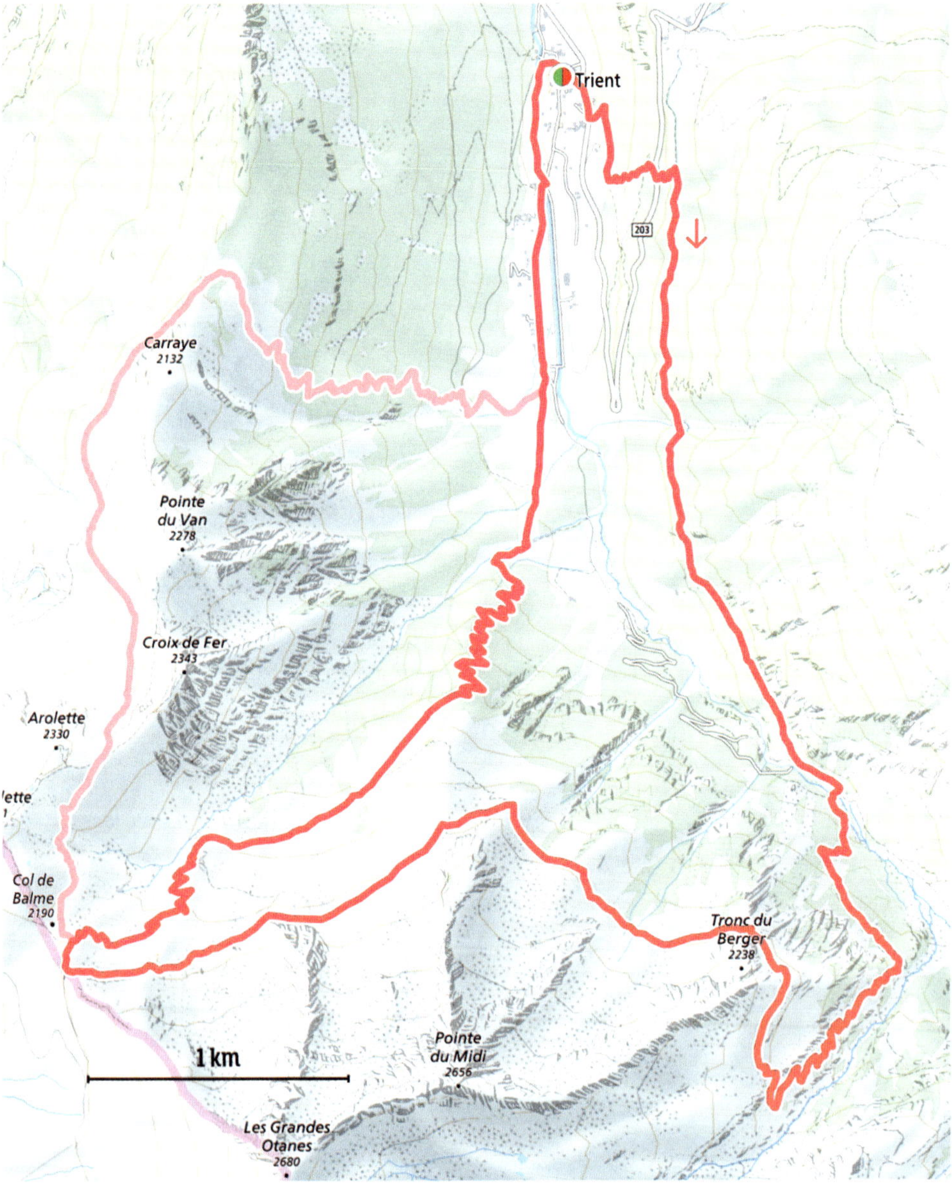
Trient
203
Carraye
2132
Pointe du Van
2278
Croix de Fer
2343
Arolette
2330
Col de Balme
2190
Tronc du Berger
2238
1 km
Pointe du Midi
2656
Les Grandes Otanes
2680

LET'S RUN!

Why we love it

The beautiful Trient Valley was carved out by the retreating glacier, and this run gives you a full tour of all the glacier left behind. This route starts up the gentle Sentier du Bisse, an old railway line from the 1800s that was used to transport glacial ice to restaurants in Paris. On the other side, you'll climb steeply up the slope before contouring around to the Col de Balme. This run is varied and adventurous and offers fantastic views of the Trient Glacier.

Getting started

From the parking lot, cross the main road and turn right to walk along the sidewalk. In 100 meters, turn left at the information board, following the yellow footpath sign. Turn left in 280 meters to ascend a steep, narrow trail through the larch trees. Continue up this trail when you hit the wide track again. Use the footbridge to cross the main road, then continue up tight switchbacks to the Sentier du Bisse.

Trient Glacier

Turn right when you reach the Sentier du Bisse and run along this gentle path for almost 2 kilometers. On your left, you'll see the Trient "bisse"—or irrigation channel—which transports glacial water to nearby meadows and vineyards. Just before the Buvette du Glacier du Trient, turn right to cross the glacial river on a wooden bridge. This icy river is the perfect place to stop and dunk your head if you're feeling the heat!

Les Grands

You'll now be following signs for Les Grands and Col de Balme. As you head away from the river, you'll be able to see the steep track up to Fenêtre d'Arpette—now on the opposite side of the valley—and you'll get increasingly clear views of the glacier. The trail comes out of the trees and traverses below a band of granite. Continue up the trail as it cuts into the rocks on a hand-built ledge. This section is exposed but not technical, and there is a handrail to help.

Col de Balme

Pass a cross and round the corner to enter a new valley. There is a small stream here, which you can use to splash your face! Follow the trail blazes around the side of Chalet

des Grands and along a rocky trail with some fixed chains. For the next kilometer, the trail is fairly rough but is clearly blazed. As you near the Col de Balme, the trail becomes more runnable, and you'll be surrounded by heather and wild blueberry bushes. You'll start to see the trail down to Trient below and to your right, and you'll see the Tête de Balme and the refuge ahead. From the col, take in stunning views of the Mont Blanc massif and the Chamonix Valley.

Final stretch

From the refuge, turn right to head back down to Trient. This first section is soft underfoot, so enjoy it while it lasts! It soon becomes rocky again until you reach the forest. Continue following signs for Trient. If you enjoy fast, absorbing descents, you will love this final forest trail! It will lead you to an open pasture, where you'll bear left and cross a river. From there, continue down to Le Peuty village. From Le Peuty, follow the road back to Trient.

Bonus kms

From the Col de Balme, continue on to Catogne d'en Haut and descend to Le Peuty via Tseppes. This adds about 1 kilometer of distance and 200 meters of vertical gain.

Pro tips

Do this run in September, when the leaves are changing color and the trails are quiet.

Finish at Refuge Le Peuty and treat yourself to an indulgent homemade burger. The refuge has an outdoor seating area facing the Trient Glacier, and if it's cold, you can sit in the cozy yurt. A visit to Refuge Le Peuty just slightly out of season allows you to fully appreciate its peaceful setting.

29 CABANE D'ORNY

A climbing run up to the Orny glacier and across to the Arpette valley via a remote mountain pass

STATISTICS

↔ Distance 16km ↑ Ascent 1375m ↓ Descent 1375m High point 2820m

DIFFICULTY

2

TECHNICALITY

COUNTRY

WHEN CAN I RUN IT?

JAN | FEB | MAR | APR | MAY | JUN | **JUL** | **AUG** | **SEP** | OCT | NOV | DEC

STYLE

60% Alpine 40% Forest Trail

POPULARITY

ACCESS

Accessible by bus. Parking is available at Télésiège de La Breya-Champex-Lac.

REFUELING

La Breya is a small restaurant with a sunny terrace that serves snacks, drinks, and a range of lunch dishes. Cabane d'Orny is a remote refuge at 2828 meters that serves basic snacks, drinks, and warm meals. Both are open between mid-June and early September.

BAIL-OUT OPTIONS

You can shorten this route by riding the La Breya chairlift up. From Cabane d'Orny, you can retrace your steps to La Breya and then ride the back down. At 12.8 kilometers, turn right to cut a corner, following signs for Champex.

RACES

Trail Verbier St-Bernard by UTMB X-Alpine

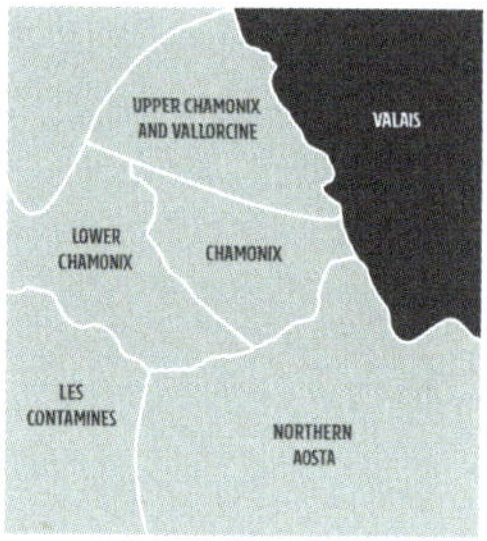
UPPER CHAMONIX AND VALLORCINE
VALAIS
LOWER CHAMONIX
CHAMONIX
LES CONTAMINES
NORTHERN AOSTA

PROFILE

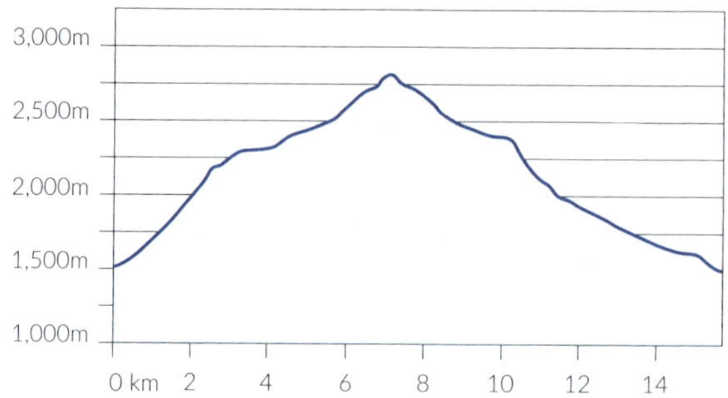
3,000m
2,500m
2,000m
1,500m
1,000m
0 km
2
4
6
8
10
12
14

Bonhomme
2436
Grand Bec
2616
Champex-Lac
Lac de Champex
Six Carro
2825
Génepi
2882
La Breya
2374
Pointe des Ecandies
2874
Petite Pointe d'Orny
3186
Aiguilles d'Arpette
Pointe d'Orny
3272
Cabane de Trient
3170
Cabane d'Orny
2828
Glacier d'Orny
Le Châtelet
2538
Tête du Vrieux
2296
Clochers du Portalet
2985
Le Portalet
3344
Roc des Plines
3294
Tête Biselx
3508
Pointe des Plines
3057
1 km
Grand Clocher des Planereuses
2804
Tête Dacier
2031
Petite Pointe des Planereuses
2965
Saleinaz

LET'S RUN!

Why we love it

This run is adventurous and varied—sections of cruisy single-track trail lead to rough, gnarly slopes. The Cabane d'Orny is a remote refuge, nestled right next to the glacier it takes its name from. It offers impressive, high-mountain views and has been offering shelter to mountaineers since 1893.

Getting started

Head up Chemin d'Arpette, following signs for Cabane d'Orny. Stay on the paved track as it rounds the corner. After 680 meters, take the second trail on your left, following a series of wooden steps and heading in the direction indicated by a yellow sign. The trail makes its way around a ski button lift, then up the slope. You'll pass through blueberry bushes and across patches of scree. After 700 meters of ascent, you'll reach the top of the Breya chairlift.

Cabane d'Orny

Go around the restaurant, then turn left up a smaller trail, following signs for Cabane d'Orny. This trail contours the rocky slope and features exposed sections, but there are fixed chains to help you. Follow trail blazes across a boulder field. At the fork, bear left to keep following signs for Cabane d'Orny. You'll soon pass over a crest; here the valley opens up and the gradient eases for a few hundred meters. Follow the trail blazes leading to the right of the impressive rock face in the middle of the valley. Soon you'll see the Cabane d'Orny ahead and the glacier to your left.

Col de la Breya

From the refuge, retrace your steps down the slope, following signs for Arpette. At around 9.5 kilometers, turn left uphill, following signs for Arpette. The trail seems to come to a dead end here, but there's a hole in the rock you can climb through. Descend briefly and then head back up to cross a small, steep gully; watch your step, as a fall here could have serious consequences. A cairn marks the top of the Col de la Breya. Follow the trail blazes down the other side and through an expanse of gray/green boulders. The trail becomes more defined and less steep before leading into the forest.

Final stretch

Turn left at the gravel track to follow signs for Arpette, then turn right at around 12.6 kilometers to head down the Arpette valley. As you emerge from the forest and enter a pasture, you'll see two wooden buildings ahead. Cross the river on a wooden bridge, then continue down the trail. Continue down the road to return to your starting point.

Bonus kms

From the Cabane d'Orny, follow signs to the Cabane du Trient. This is an adventurous out-and-back add-on that follows the rocky trails along the side of the glacier. The out-and-back to the Cabane du Trient will add 4 kilometers and 350 meters of climbing and descending.

Pro tips

There are no water fountains on this route, and there is rarely running water. Make sure to bring plenty of water with you. You can buy bottled water from Restaurant la Breya and Cabane d'Orny when they are open, and if you have a water filter, you can fill up your flask from the lake just behind the refuge.

Stop for a warm meal, snack, or drink at the Cabane d'Orny. The team here serves a range of basic, comforting mountain-fare such as omelettes, rösti, and soup.

Turn this into a multi-day adventure by staying the night at the Cabane d'Orny or the Cabane du Trient.

30 FENÊTRE D'ARPETTE

A challenging circular route that climbs up the side of the Trient Glacier and then cuts down to the beautiful Arpette valley

STATISTICS

Distance 26km | Ascent 1910m | Descent 1910m | High point 2662m

DIFFICULTY

3

TECHNICALITY

COUNTRY

WHEN CAN I RUN IT?

JAN FEB MAR APR MAY JUN **JUL AUG SEP** OCT NOV DEC

STYLE

80% Alpine 10% Forest Trail 10% Road

POPULARITY

ACCESS

Accessible by bus. There is a parking area on the Col de la Forclaz, on the opposite side of the road from Hôtel du Col de la Forclaz.

REFUELING

Buvette du Glacier du Trient and the Alpage de Bovine serve a range of drinks, lunches, snacks, and homemade cakes. Both are open from June to early September. La Gentiana bakery on the main street of Champex sells sandwiches, quiches, and patisseries and is open year-round.

BAIL-OUT OPTIONS

There are no easy ways to shorten this route. From Champex you could get back to the Col de la Forclaz by taking the bus to Orsières, followed by the train to Martigny, then bus up to the Col.

RACES

UTMB Mont-Blanc
UTMB Mont-Blanc CCC
UTMB Mont-Blanc OCC
UTMB Mont-Blanc MCC

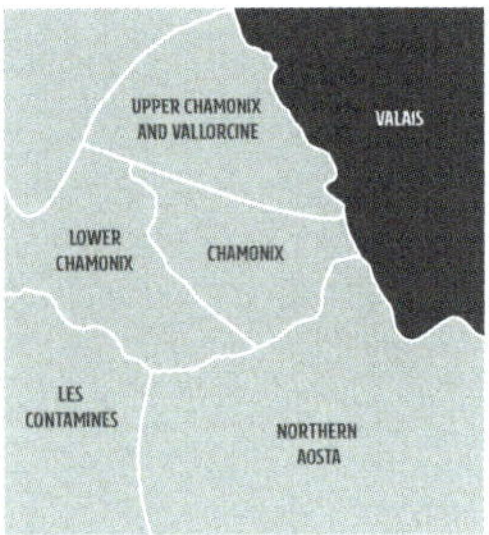
UPPER CHAMONIX AND VALLORCINE
VALAIS
LOWER CHAMONIX
CHAMONIX
LES CONTAMINES
NORTHERN AOSTA

PROFILE

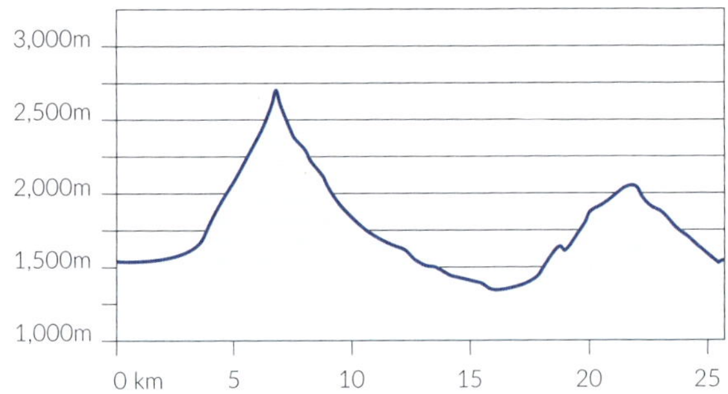
3,000m
2,500m
2,000m
1,500m
1,000m
0 km
5
10
15
20
25

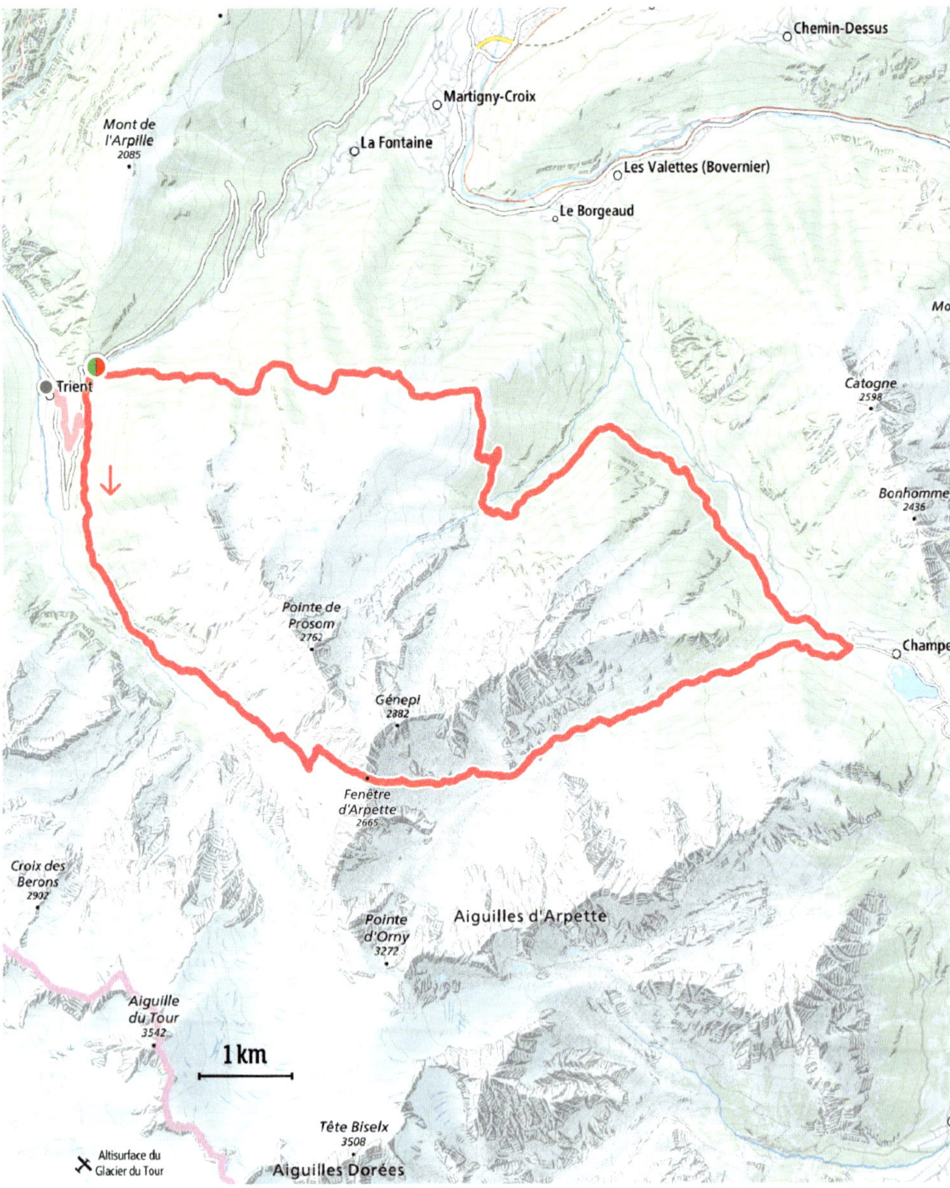
Chemin-Dessus
Martigny-Croix
Mont de l'Arpille 2085
La Fontaine
Les Valettes (Bovernier)
Le Borgeaud
Trient
Catogne 2598
Bonhomme 2436
Pointe de Prosom 2762
Champex
Génepi 2882
Fenêtre d'Arpette 2665
Croix des Berons 2902
Pointe d'Orny 3272
Aiguilles d'Arpette
Aiguille du Tour 3542
1 km
Tête Biselx 3508
Altisurface du Glacier du Tour
Aiguilles Dorées

LET'S RUN!

Why we love it

This run climbs up to the Fenêtre d'Arpette, a stunning mountain pass on the side of the Trient glacier. The route follows remote, adventurous trails and offers fantastic views.

Getting started

Start opposite the hotel and take the footpath signed for Trient. After a few hundred meters, cross a wooden bridge and follow the flat, shady trail for 3 kilometers until you reach Buvette du Glacier du Trient. Just past the buvette, take the trail that bears left, marked by blazes.

Vésevey Hunting Cabin

At around 4.4 kilometers, the trail becomes narrow and exposed and there's a fixed rope to hold onto. This section is new and was built to circumvent a landslide that did away with the original trail. A little further on, you'll come to a small, privately-owned hunters' cabin, which is a great place to take a breather.

Fenêtre d'Arpette

From the cabin, follow the blazes on your left, which direct you up steep boulder fields and patches of scree. The top of the pass is often cold due to strong glacial winds, but there are plenty of boulders to shelter behind.

Val d'Arpette

Pick your way down the other side of the pass, following trail blazes and signs for Arpette. After descending 300 vertical meters, the trail becomes more defined. Cross a stream and bear left at the forks to continue heading downhill. Pass through the Arpette pasture, then head down the paved road until you reach the main road in Champex.

Alpage de Bovine

Turn left onto the main road and follow it for 500 meters. Look for a large rock, onto which someone has painted "Bovine" and "TMB." Turn left and follow the gravel track for 1 kilometer. At around 14.4 kilometers, bear left to leave the main Tour du Mont Blanc route and follow a smaller trail into the forest. Turn left at the next intersection, following signs for Bovine. A series of steep switchbacks leads you up through the forest and out onto a working pasture.

Final stretch

From the Alpage de Bovine buvette, follow the main trail as it climbs 50 meters to a small gate, where you'll have a wide-open view of the Rhône valley below. The final descent is on fairly smooth, runnable forest trails.

Bonus kms

Add 4 kilometers and 227 meters of ascent by starting and finishing your run in Trient.

Pro tips

There is often snow lingering on the east side of the Fenêtre d'Arpette, so be careful when crossing snow bridges. Do this route later in the season if you're uncomfortable crossing snowfields.

Do not go over the Fenêtre d'Arpette in bad weather, as there is no shelter nearby.

Treat yourself to a celebratory rösti or homemade cake at the Alpage de Bovine, which is not far from the end of the run.

WITH THANKS

This guide is the result of the collective efforts of the Run the Alps crew and our friends. Charlie Edwards, Emily Geldard, Hillary Gerardi, and Doug Mayer were at the heart of this project and worked on the book you have in your hands from inception to publication.

Any errors or omissions are entirely our responsibility. Should you find anything that needs correction, please let us know! You can email us anytime at guidebook@runthealps.com.

The photography for this project was overseen by Sam Hill. This book also features the work of Dan Fitzgerald, Nick Danielson, Toni Spasenoski, and Milo Zanecchia.

The run models include: Kieren Dsouza, Chris Edwards, Emily Edwards, Jana Gibalova, Val Stori, Mirna Valerio, Georgie Fitzgerald, Mimmi Kotka, Marleen de Graff, Elaine Ginger, Matthew Breakell, Kristians Lunins, Scott Cornish, Hannah Mawdsley, Ted Toussaint, Leigh-Anne Burns, Suzanne Evans, Cristina Podocea, Rosanna Gooder, Sheridan Stride, and Leo Pinnock.

Additional thanks to Angelos Adamakopoulos, Corrado and Mara Borghesio, Carrie Craig, Chris and Emily Edwards, Simon James, José Mattijssen, Alberto and Erica Motta, Holly Page, Becki Penrose, Alix Pico, Astrid Renet, and Giles Ruck for their helpful contributions.

Thanks to all the guides, staff, and friends of Run the Alps, whose collective wisdom fills these pages.

We are grateful to have been able to work with Helvetiq, one of Europe's best publishing houses. Thanks to Hadi Barkat, Richard Harvell, Sonia Curtis, and Daniel Malak.